CW01558050

Journal of

The Colloquium for Information System Security Education (CISSE)

October 2017

CISSE Edition 5, Issue 1

Please contact us at *askCISSE@cisse.info*

www.cisse.info

Table of Contents

Editor's Comments

For twenty-one years, the Colloquium for Information System Security Education (CISSE) has been the sole forum in which the members of the academic field of cybersecurity have gathered to present and discuss new ideas. CISSE was first established to provide a single place to conduct productive conversations between a variety of government, industry, and academic on the topic of cybersecurity education. Ideas arising from those discussions have led to new and improved content and curricula for cybersecurity teaching.

The academic community meets every year at a different part of the Country to present and discuss the most effective means for maintaining a high standard of excellence in cybersecurity education. As a way of ensuring continuing excellence in the field, new and evolving knowledge contributions are presented to the membership. We consider it our duty to ensure the highest academic standards for these presentations.

In our opinion, the contributions to this journal represent the best possible current scholarship in the field of cybersecurity and their selection and inclusion is highly competitive. It is the aim of this Journal to offer only the most outstanding research available. However, the editors and publishers also work with new authors to help them to bring their work to publishable standards.

In that respect, the papers submitted to the conference undergo a rigorous double-blind refereeing process and the contributions that are deemed the most outstanding are presented in individual sessions at the Conference. Once the Conference is ended an Editorial Board selects a small set of the papers that contain meaningful and innovative ideas for presentation to the community at-large. These are the ideas that you will discover in this Journal.

Given that background it should be understood that the ideas contained in this Journal are considered to be the most painstakingly thought through recommendations with respect to methods and practices for cybersecurity teaching. Cybersecurity is an emerging discipline. And make no mistake, it IS a holistic discipline, separate from any of the conventional computer studies. Thus, it is critical to publicize the broadest and most comprehensive range of persuasive new ideas about where the discipline will evolve going forward.

Therefore, the ideas presented here are not constrained by any preconceived notions of what the field ought to be like. Instead we are focusing on their merit as a means of solving difficult problems that exist in our modern society. That is the case because there are many systemic and cultural challenges that have to be overcome before we can get a holistic understanding of this critical field. Our goal is to present every point of view.

The articles in this Journal address ways to more effectively leverage the range of sub- disciplines in the defense of an organization. Spreading the net as wide as possible is a particularly obvious and justifiable way to address threat. And that is our mandate and challenge to the researchers, and cybersecurity professionals of the future.

Effective strategies for protecting the organization against relevant electronic, human and physical threat require understanding the state of the various existing common communities that comprise the educational landscape. The contents of this Journal focus on developing and maintaining insight into every legitimate approach to cybersecurity. We will present the wide range of approaches and provide solutions in the form of up-to-date ideas about ensuring a continuously capable response. We will focus on best practices for practical education and training for the modem cybersecurity profession as well as transformative thinking for the profession as a whole.

What you will find in this issue are ten carefully selected articles that discuss aspects of existing ideas or new issues that are arising. The articles here represent many avenues of thought. It is our considered opinion that this sort of wide-ranging dialogue constitutes the first steps in overcoming the silo effect that has hampered the field from its inception. We are dedicated to taking the first steps in ensuring that cybersecurity education evolves into the kind of main tent profession that we all want it to be. We would not have been able to do this alone, and so we would like to acknowledge Tamara Shoemaker for her outstanding work in managing the review and production process, and our colleagues who served as reviewers for this issue:

Paul Beard, Christopher Brew, Steven Brown, Yuntai Chang, Ankur Chattopadhyay, Joseph Ekstrom, Chani El Kari, Erik Fretheim, Eric Hulderson, Yesem Kurt-Peker, Derek Manwaring, Themis Papageorge, Julio Perez, Jason Pittman, Huw Owain Lyndon Read, Ken Sigler, Paul Wang, Kevin Wu, and Koukeng Yang.

Editor

Dan Shoemaker, Ph.D., Professor and Graduate Program Director
University of Detroit Mercy

Editor CISSE Journal

Paper of the Year for 2017

Academic Influence of Social Network Sites on the Collegiate Performance of Technical College Students

Jameson McFarlane ★
mcfarlane@stevenscollege.edu

Thorne J. McFarlane ★★
tmcfar17@jhu.edu

Leon Bernard ★★★
lberna1@students.towson.edu

★ Thaddeus Stevens College;
★★ Johns Hopkins University;
★★★ Towson University

750 E. King Street Lancaster, PA 17602; 3400 N. Charles Street, Baltimore, MD 21218; 8000 York Road, Towson, MD 21252

Abstract - Social network sites (SNS) is an emerging phenomenon that is here to stay. The popularity and the ubiquity of the SNS technology is undeniable. Because most SNS are free and easy to use people from all walks of life and from almost any age are attracted to that technology. College age students are by far the largest segment of the population using SNS. Since most SNS have been adapted for mobile devices, not only do you find students using this technology in their study, while working on labs or on projects, a substantial number of students have been found to use SNS even while listening to lecture. This study found that SNS use has a significant negative impact on the grade point average of college students particularly in the first semester. However, this negative impact is greatly diminished by the end of the third semester partly because the students have adjusted satisfactorily to the challenges of college or because they have learned how to adequately manage their time. It was established that the kinds of activities the students are engaged in during the SNS use are the leading factor affecting academic performance. Of those activities, using SNS during a lecture or while studying is the foremost contributing factor to lower academic performance. This is due to "cognitive" or "information" bottleneck, a condition in which the students find it very difficult to multitask or to switch between resources leading to inefficiency in information retention and thus, educational performance.

Categories and Subject Descriptors

K.3.2 [Computers and Education]: *Computer and Information Science Education*

General Terms

Social network analysis, Security, regression analysis, Grade Point Average

Keywords

Social network sites, social network analysis, correlation of determinants, correlation of coefficient, regression coefficient, cognitive dissonance, psychological engagement, f-statistic

1   INTRODUCTION

Although social network sites (SNS) have been around since 1997 [1], it wasn't until 2005 - 2006 when Facebook was introduced to the rest of the world for anyone with an email address that we saw an exponential proliferation in the number of people who adopted, explored and used this social service [1], [2]. Since then, SNS, has become ubiquitous with a projected three billion users world-wide to be connected to SNS by 2020 [3]. Whereas the world's top five SNS are Facebook, YouTube, Instagram, Twitter and [3], in North America, the top SNS are Facebook, Instagram, Pinterest, Twitter and LinkedIn [4]. In the United States, Facebook account for seventy-nine percent of all users of SNS [4]. Further in the United States, the majority of the people who use SNS are individuals between ages 18 and 29 (88 percent of users) who possess some level of college education (82 percent of users) [4], [5].

SNS are platforms that allow users to share all sorts of information about themselves, their friends and families; to keep in contact with new people; to share files, load and upload pictures, share links and other pertinent information that their followers or friends might find it useful to know [6], [7]. SNA data can be downloaded and analyzed to produce a treasure trove of information for researchers and academics alike who are interested in studying the characteristics of social groups, an area known as social network analysis (SNA).

Social network analysis has been used in the past to determine what impact, if any that SNS use have on the academic performance or grade point average (GPA) of college students. Several researchers have found that SNS use by students have a net positive effect on the GPA of college students [8], [9]. Other researchers have determined that the use of SNS significantly negatively impacts the GPA of college students as a lack of student engagement as well as multitasking and switching which reduces a person's cognitive resources to accomplish a diversity of tasks successfully [10] − [15]. Still further studies have established no correlation whatsoever between college students' grades and the use of social network sites like Facebook [16], [17].

Numerous studies have already been done on the dynamics that affect college students' grade point average especially in their freshman year when they are most vulnerable to academic success or student attrition. Among other variables, there is empirical evidence to prove high school grade point average (HSGPA) is one of the key predictors of academic performance of first year college students [18] − [20]. Meanwhile, other factors that could impact college GPA include: academic self-efficacy and optimism [21]; achievement motivators [22]; student engagement [8], [9], [23], [24]; and even differing pedagogical approaches to teaching in the high schools [25].

Past studies on the impact of social network sites (SNS) and academic performance of college students have focused primarily on four-year colleges except for a study by Evans et al. that was implemented in a community college environment [26]. However, there has not been any research work to date to determine if a correlation exists between high school grade point average and the use of SNS in two-year technical colleges. This study is an attempt to fill that gap.

In this study, the focus is on whether a college student's academic performance is affected by the usage of social network sites. While there is empirical data supporting high school grade point average, Facebook usage and college academic performance, the use of other social network sites are yet to be established.

The primary objectives of this study are:

R1: *Does the use of SNS impact the academic GPA of students in the first two years of college?*

R2: *Does the amount of time students use SNS impact their GPA?*

R3: *Does the kind of activity students are engaged in while using SNS affect their academic performance in the classroom*

2   LITERATURE REVIEW

In this section, an overview of the various factors that can be used to predict a student's academic grade point average in college is presented. This is absolutely important specifically because college students are most vulnerable to dropping out and student attrition in their first two years of college.

There are a significant number of factors that impact the academic performance of college students. For the purpose of this study, the impact of academic performance on college is examined. Then, an overview of the influence of student engagement to learning is presented. Finally, SNS is evaluated to determine its effect on learning.

2.1 Predicting College of Academic GPA

2.1.1 Academic Performance

A substantial amount of work has been done on academic success in high school, performance on standardized tests, and its association with students' academic success in college along with student attrition. These studies have found that both high school academic success and the scores on standardized tests are two of the most significant predictors of success in college [20], [21], [27] – [30]. A study by Johnson and Wolfe found that high school grade point average, SAT scores and self-control account for 19%, 5% and 9% of the variance of college GPA, respectively [31]. Zwick and Sklar did a similar study on minority students which yielded similar results [32]. However, Camara and Michaelides believe that with so many high school students currently having GPAs reaching in excess of 4.0, standardized exams have thus become more reliable and valid in predicting students' academic success in college [19], [33].

2.1.2 Student Engagement

In a cross-sectional review of many of the research studies relating to success of college students, Braxton concluded that there are eight domains of indicators of student success in college [34]. These include: academic attainment [24], [35]; acquisition of general education [36]; development of academic competence [37]; development of cognitive skills and intellectual dispositions [8]; occupational attainment [38]; preparation of adulthood and citizenship [37]; personal accomplishments [39]; and personal development [8].

Kuh and his colleagues were challenged by the National Postsecondary Education Cooperative to review the literature and to compile a report that would provide an informed perspective on policies, programs and best practices that can make a difference to acceptable student performance in postsecondary education [40], [41]. They proposed that success in postsecondary education be defined broadly by academic achievement, engagement in educationally purposeful activities, satisfaction, acquisition of desired knowledge, skills and competencies, persistence, attainment of educational objectives, and post college performance [9].

It is imperative to observe that student engagement is an overarching, overriding dynamic to student success in college. Student engagement can be described as the time and effort students devote to activities that are "empirically linked" to desired learning outcomes and objectives [41]. Research has shown that students gained more from their studies when they devote more time and energy to the task at hand [8], [24], [35], [41], [42]. The time spent on tasks was underscored by Astin in a longitudinal study of student development dubbed "student involvement theory" in which he posits that the greater the quality and quantity of the physical and psychological energy a student invests in his college experience the greater the amount of student learning and personal development [24], [35], [39].

2.1.3 Social Networking Sites (SNS) and learning

SNS is ubiquitous. It is predominantly common among 18 – 29-year olds [4], [43]. Facebook has become the defacto SNS of choice for college students [4], [44], [45]. Not only do college students spend an appreciable amount of time on these SNS at their homes and dorms, they also surreptitiously use SNS in the classroom. Some professors have resorted to banning the use of social media in the classroom because they believe it is detrimental to learning in the classroom. Other professors are unable to ban the use in the classroom and as such have reluctantly resorted to incorporating the technology in the classroom learning environment.

With the proliferation of SNS among high school and college students, a significant amount of research has been done to examine the impact that SNS usage has on the academic performance of these students. Kirschner and

Karpinski found that non-Facebook users had reported a higher-grade point average (GPA) than Facebook users [13]. They believed this was due to poor time management skills by the students, although Alloway surmised that SNS use innately creates a proclivity to procrastinate [46]. Junco also compared SNS usage and college GPA. Junco found a significantly negative relationship between time spent on Facebook and freshman GPA [5], [10], [11], [47]. In addition, it was found that there is an association between the kind of activities and GPA [47]. Ophir observed that switching (multitasking) requires a person to juggle his or her limited cognitive resources to accomplish the different task successfully which leads to greater inefficiency [12]. In a related study, Fox et al. found a negative relationship between students who IMing and reading comprehension and overall GPA. They found that the more time students spend on Instant Messaging (IM) the lower their reading scores and consequently, the lower their GPA [48]. The lowering comprehension can be comparable to texting whilst driving.

Further, a number of researchers have linked the use of SNS and GPA to the negative effects of multitasking [10], [14], [15], [47]. Fried [15] and Lauricella [14] suggested that considerable multitasking on off task activities considerably affect student learning. Other researchers have penned this multitasking effect as "cognitive bottleneck". Cognitive bottleneck or information bottleneck is a constraint in which one focuses on more than one activity at a time. This interferes with memory decisions and often leads to memory leakage or forgetting and redoing of associated tasks [49] – [52]. This can negatively impact student grades.

3   RESEARCH DESIGN

In this section, a description of the participants along with how the data obtained for publication was gathered.

3.1 Participants

From 2014 – 17 Thaddeus Stevens College of Technology (TSCT) has been named and or awarded the Aspen Prize for Excellence as the top two-year college in Pennsylvania as well as one of the top 150 in the country [53]. The student population is primarily from the lower socio-economic status (SES) and the majority of the students live on campus. A total of 150 students from over 18 programs voluntarily participated in the online survey. The students were not offered any incentives to complete the survey. They were also reminded that their participation is voluntary as an analysis of the survey results will be published.

By a significant margin, the students in the survey primarily used Facebook and YouTube in both high school and college. More students in college used Instagram and LinkedIn than in high school (see Figure 1 and Figure 2 below).

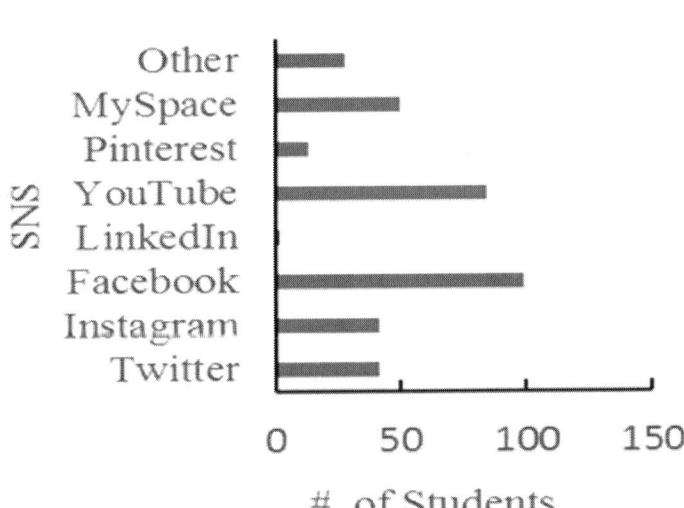

Figure 1: SNS Used in High School

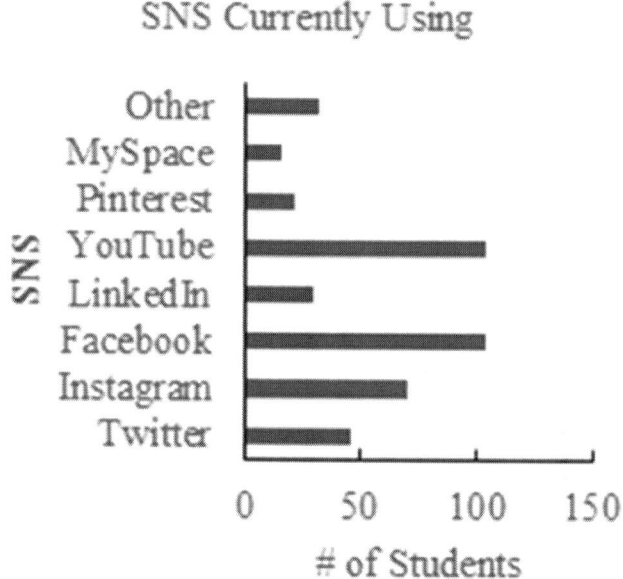

Figure 2: SNS Use in College

3.2 Research Design

The survey consisted of 16 multiple choice / multiple grid questions. It was created and designed using Google Forms. The survey questions addressed 11 different areas including: SNS usage; names of SNS websites used; how frequently they use SNS websites; the amount of time spent daily on SNS; how often they use their mobile phones to visit SNS during lecture; do they have special times for using and visiting SNS; their academic GPA at the end of high school and that of the first three semesters of college; do they have specific reasons for using SNS; and what is their age, gender and ethnicity.

Once the survey was completed, the data was downloaded into an excel spreadsheet for analysis. Upon the data download and cleansing, r programming was used for the data visualization. In all, 142 students from 18 programs responded to the survey. Eighty-four percent of the respondents were males,

13

which is typical of the technical college. In other to determine whether the students' academic grades had declined or not, each student was asked to provide a range for the high school grade point average (HSGPA) as well as the range for their college academic GPA for their first three semesters at TSCT. Table 1 below gives a summary of the students' academic GPA.

# of Participants	Academic Grade Point Average			
	< 1.99	2.0 – 2.64	2.7 – 3.64	3.7 – 4.0
HSGPA	5	24	83	30
Semester 1	2	22	69	49
Semester 2	3	23	74	42
Semester 3	4	26	72	40

Table 1: Summary of Participants and GPA

3.3 Procedure

At the beginning of the spring semester (January, 2017) an email was sent to a certain number of the sophomore college faculty informing them of the survey and the need to encourage their students to participate in it. They were asked to allow the students 20 minutes of their time to complete the 16-item questionnaire between February 13 and 24. The survey was created using Google Forms. Once the form was completed, a hyperlink was generated. This hyperlink was included in an email addressed to the faculty of the various programs on January 27. Once the due date had expired, the data was downloaded to an .xls file for processing. Numeric values or attributes were given to the responses to determine whether correlations existed. Regression analysis and data visualizations were then calculated using r programming.

4 EXPERIMENTAL RESULTS AND DISCUSSION

4.1 Does the use of SNS impact the academic GPA of student in the first two years of college?

Here six different responses were analyzed to determine the academic impact through the end of the first semester in their sophomore year. The six different responses include: whether or not they have SNS accounts; did they use SNS in high school; what current SNS they are using; how often they visit these SNS; when were they introduced to SNS and; for how long they have been using SNS.

Using the linear model for the HSGPA, we observed a highly significant Pr $(> |t|)$ value and high t-value (15.819). As a result, the null hypotheses should be rejected. The F-distribution of 1.767 also implies that there is a relationship between HSPGA and SNS use. The main factors that affect the GPA are the number of SNS sites visited and, to a lesser extent, when the students were introduced to SNS. However, because the coefficient of determination ($r2$) is so small (0.07283), then the strength of the association between the variables is not very strong.

```
Coefficients:
            Estimate Std. Error t value Pr(>|t|)
(Intercept)  3.43356    0.19804  17.337  <2e-16 ***
HAS.SNS      0.17558    0.11016   1.594  0.1133
CURR.SITES   0.07822    0.04219   1.854  0.0659 .
HS.SITES    -0.08735    0.04534  -1.926  0.0562 .
REGULAR      0.02857    0.03444   0.829  0.4083
INTRO       -0.08000    0.04079  -1.961  0.0519 .
YEARS       -0.08528    0.06961  -1.225  0.2226
---
Signif. codes:  0 '***' 0.001 '**' 0.01 '*' 0.05 '.' 0.1 ' ' 1

Residual standard error: 0.525 on 135 degrees of freedom
Multiple R-squared:  0.08541,   Adjusted R-squared:  0.04476
F-statistic: 2.101 on 6 and 135 DF,  p-value: 0.05706
```

Figure 3: Freshman 1st Semester Linear Model

Figure 3 above presents the regression model for the first college semester. It can be observed that a correlation exists between SNS use and academic grade point average in each semester. It should be noted however, that the coefficient of determination and the F-distribution is larger in the first semester of college than any of the other semesters. This implies that there is a stronger correlation in the first semester of college. In addition, the p-value is also smaller in the first semester than the other semesters as well, which confirms our assumption. It should be noted that by the end of the third semester in college, the strength of the association is marginally significant at all. In fact, a close examination of the residual graphs for each of the semesters depicts a regular pattern and a residual centered on the mean. By far, the best pattern is between high school and the first semester which is a clear indication of the existence of a correlation between the variables.

4.2 Does the amount of time students use SNS impact their GPA?

Here, the goal is to determine the regularity of the respondents' visits to the SNS, how much time they spend on the social networking sites per day, and how frequently they visit the SNS per week and its impact on academic grade point average. In addition, the ratings the respondents provided of their SNS use over the past year is also used in the calculation. Table 2 below offers a synopsis of the coefficient results.

GPA	t value	Standard Error	R^2	F-statistics	p-value
HS	25.131	0.13194	0.02595	1.226	0.3028
1st Semester	25.729	0.12856	0.02348	1.106	0.349
2nd Semester	24.780	0.13169	0.00701	0.3247	0.8075
3rd Semester	22.601	0.13696	0.02466	1.163	0.3263

Table 2: Coefficient Values

Overall, a correlation exists between academic grade point average and the regularity of the student visit on social networking sites. A close examination of Table 2, illustrates slightly large p-values. This is a clear indication that the correlation between the response variables and the predictor is not vastly significant. It can be perceived by the large 0.8075 p-value of the SNS in the second college semester that SNS does not reflect any significance in the respondents' academic grade point average. Further, the small values of the r2 undoubtedly attest to a weak correlation among the variables. For example, the r-squared value for the second semester is 0.00701 which is relatively low in comparison with the other semesters. What is most intriguing is that the SNS correlation in the second college semester is considerably weaker than that of the third semester. It can will be observed that all except the residuals for the third semester depict nearly straight lines with no residuals centered on the mean. This is a strong indication of a poor fit – in other words there is no strong correlation.

4.3 Does the kind of Activity the students are engaged in while using SNS affect academic performance in the classroom?

In this section, the kinds of activities the students are engaged in while using SNS is examined to determine whether it has a detrimental effect on the learning process in the classroom. Specifically, SNS use is analyzed to establish if it has any impact on the students' studying habits and their aptitude to retain information at the same time, because the capability of the student to study effectively have a significant influence on their college academic performance. It is imperative to comprehend whether the seemingly insidious habit of using SNS during lectures might be more detrimental to learning in the classroom than we anticipated.

Using a linear regression model, it can be observed that a high degree of correlation exists between the activities and academic performance at the high school level. Specifically, using SNS during lecture or at special times have the highest negative influence on academic GPA. Further, an increase in the frequency of SNS use or even increases in the use of SNS during lecture or while studying will cause an inverse but reduction in the HSGPA. With the high F-statistic (2.085), it is concluded that a correlation exists as well. However, due to the small coefficient of determination (0.098), it can be deduced that the strength of the association between SNS use and academic performance is relatively low. In the second semester, based on the small standard error values along with the values for the F-statistic and the p-value for the t-test, it can be fairly formulated that the coefficients are significant for the model. As such, there is a level of correlation between the dependent and independent variables.

However, the most substantial activities that affect academic performance appear to be using SNS during a lecture and while studying.

In the third semester of college, the coefficient figures for the activities are significantly different when compared to the second semester. Whereas a correlation exists in both semesters, it can be observed that the F-statistics and the r2 for the third semester is substantially larger than that of the second semester. This suggests that the association between the relationships is more significant in the third semester and that the strength of this association is also stronger in the third semester than the second semester. Furthermore, the p-value in the second semester (0.7059) is more than twice the size of that in the third semester (0.3224), again demonstrating that the relationship is more meaningful in the third semester compared to that of the second semester.

5 DISCUSSION, IMPLICATIONS, LIMITATIONS AND CONCLUSION

5.1 Discussion

Overall, the results of the study provide empirical evidence that a correlation exists between college students' SNS use and their academic performance. Based on the analysis of the results, the impact of SNS on academic GPA is greatest in the first semester and is very minimal by the end of the third semester of college. In general, the results highlighted the kinds of activities the students are engaged in while using SNS is a crucial aspect in their academic grade point average. Below is a discussion of the research results.

5.1.1 Research Question I
R1: *Does the use of SNS impact the academic GPA of students in the first two years of college?*

The analysis of the research illustrates a positive correlation between the use of SNS and student academic performance from high school to college. However, it was found that the strength between grade point averages and the other independent variables were stronger in the first semester of college compared to the third semester. In fact, by the end of the third college semester, the impact of SNS on academic performance is relatively non-existent. A possible explanation for this phenomenon could be that the students are becoming more comfortable with the social network technology while also adjusting to the college environment. Most importantly, it is not just having an SNS account that have the greatest impact on students' grades but rather it is when they were introduced to SNS, the kind of site they are using as well as how regularly they visit the sites.

5.1.2 Research Question 2

R2: *Does the amount of time students use SNS impact their GPA?*

The results of the study confirm that the more time the students spend on SNS the lower their academic performance. This can be attributed to poor time management skills and a propensity to procrastinate [5], [10], [11], [46]. This is more critical in the students' first semester of college as they have to learn to adjust to the higher level of work, different studying habits and overall more or frequent assignments. But the amount of time used on SNS is less of a factor in the second semester as compared to the first and third semesters of college. This could be because the students might be using SNS less regularly or they have more time to concentrate on their school work or they have adjusted to the rigors of the college environment.

5.1.3 Research Question 3

R3: *Does the kind of activity the students are engaged in while using SNS affect their academic performance in the classroom?*

The analysis of the results provide empirical evidence that the kind of activities the students are engaged in during SNS use has a significant effect on the academic performances of the college students. For instance, using SNS while working on labs or on projects does not have any major impact on learning. However, using SNS during a lecture or while studying have a more profound influence on academic grade point average because it calls for higher student engagement and involvement. Further, using SNS in a lecture calls for a greater level of multitasking and switching on the student's cognitive capacities [12], [24], [43].

5.2 Implications

The results of the study provide supportive evidence for previous research [10], [11], [13], [46], [47], [54] on the negative impact of SNS use on the academic performance of college students. This negative impact is greater during the first couple of semesters of college, in particular the first semester, as the students grapple with the rigors of study and their new environments. By the end of the third semester of college, there is very little effect of SNS on academic performance. However, it is the activities that students are engaged during SNS use that significantly affect their grade point average. For example, using SNS during lectures have a negative effect on learning as well as academic performance.

Since students spend two years in most technical colleges (and community colleges as well), it is imperative that college faculty and administrators understand this inhibitor to academic performance and to provide an environment whereby the students' grades will not falter during the course of their studies because, unlike a four-year college, they have very little time to restore and improve their grade point once it has fallen. Furthermore, prior to their graduation, college students are supposed to receive and demonstrate a certain level of skills to make them productive citizens. If they are not reaching that level of competency and proficiency in the necessary areas, then the system has failed them.

Further, it can be very helpful if faculty can provide opportunities to utilize SNS in the teaching learning activities. That way, students would be less likely to use SNS in the classroom where the impact of SNS is most noticeably negative.

5.3 Limitations

There are some limitations to this study. First of all, the sample size of the research study is very small and the environment may be different from many other colleges. Moreover, the study was done with a limited number of college sophomores. The study could yield different results if a larger number of students from a cross sectional colleges is surveyed.

Furthermore, some students take harder classes and their major is more difficult than others. In addition, some faculty provide a better methodology for student engagement and learning than others. Hence, a student's academic performance can be an overarching attitude of teaching in the classroom, the student's ability, peer tutoring, and so on, and not the use of the SNS technology per se.

5.4 Conclusion

Social network sites are an emerging phenomenon that is here to stay. The popularity and ubiquity of the SNS technology is undeniable. As the technology continues to grow we may well see a convergence of the technology with teaching methodologies in the classrooms. Moreover, as students find more and generic uses of these applications, it is likely that this technology will continue to compete with college students' activities for learning and how they prepare for their classes; the structure, methodology and the approach utilized by the faculty in making the teaching and learning environment most constructive and conducive for the students; and of course, the benefits and the academic output that these students yielded from the combinations of all these emergent systems. It behooves college faculty and educational administrators to factor this SNS technology into their strategic planning in order to maximize the students' potential to design a learning that is more complete and productive.

Since two-year technical college students amass all the knowledge and skills to make them productive employees within four semesters, it is highly important that college administrators understand the factors affecting student performance in the classroom and develop means to mitigate these elements. Not only is this important for learning but it is also very critical for student college retention, an area that continues to plague both two- and four-year colleges.

REFERENCES

[1] N. B. Ellison, "Social Network Sites: Definition, History, and Scholarship."

[2] S. Griffith, "An introduction to the potential of social networking sites in education," *Emerg. Technol. Conf. 2008*, no. June, pp. 18–21, 2008.

[3] N. Johnson, "The Top 15 Most Popular Social-Media Sites in 2016 [Infographic]," *Plugingroup*, 2016. [Online]. Available: https://plugingroup.com/top-15-popular-social-media-sites-november-2016/. [Accessed: 06-Feb-2017].

[4] M. Duggan, D. Page, and S. C. Manager, "Social Media Update 2016," *Pew Res. Cent.*, no. November, 2016.

[5] R. Junco, "The relationship between frequency of Facebook use, participation in Facebook activities, and student engagement," *Comput. Educ.*, vol. 58, no. 1, pp. 162–171, 2012.

[6] P. B. Brandtzæg and J. Heim, "Why People Use Social Networking Sites," *Online communities Soc. Comput.*, pp. 143–152, 2009.

[7] K. Y. Lin and H. P. Lu, "Why people use social networking sites: An empirical study integrating network externalities and motivation theory," *Comput. Human Behav.*, vol. 27, no. 3, pp. 1152–1161, 2011.

[8] E. T. Pascarella and P. T. Terenzini, "How college affects students: A third decade of research.," *How College Affects Students: A Third Decade of Research.* pp. 534–545, 2005.

[9] G. D. Kuh, T. M. Cruce, R. Shoup, J. Kinzie, and R. M. Gonyea, "Unmasking the Effects of Student on First-Year College Engagement Grades and Persistence," *J. Higher Educ.*, vol. 79, no. 5, pp. 540–563, 2008.

[10] R. Junco and S. R. Cotten, "No A 4 U: The relationship between multitasking and academic performance," *Comput. Educ.*, vol. 59, no. 2, pp. 505–514, 2012.

[11] R. Junco, "Student class standing, Facebook use, and academic performance," *J. Appl. Dev. Psychol.*, vol. 36, pp. 18–29, 2015.

[12] E. Ophir, C. Nass, and A. D. Wagner, "Cognitive control in media multitaskers," *Proc. Natl. Acad. Sci.*, vol. 106, no. 37, pp. 15583–15587, 2009.

[13] P. A. Kirschner and A. C. Karpinski, "Facebook?? and academic performance," *Comput. Human Behav.*, vol. 26, no. 6, pp. 1237–1245, 2010.

[14] R. H. Kay and S. Lauricella, "Unstructured vs. Structured Use of Laptops in Higher Education," *J. Inf. Technol. Educ.*, vol. 10, pp. 33–42, 2011.

[15] C. B. Fried, "In-class laptop use and its effects on student learning," *Comput. Educ.*, vol. 50, no. 3, pp. 906–914, 2008.

[16] E. a Kolek and D. Saunders, "Online Disclosure: An Empirical Examination of Undergraduate Facebook Profiles," *J. Stud. Aff. Res. Pract.*, vol. 45, no. 1, pp. 1–25, 2008.

[17] J. Pasek and E. Hargittai, "Facebook and academic performance: Reconciling a media sensation with data," *First Monday*, vol. 14, no. 5, pp. 1–14, 2009.

[18] M. A. Conard, "Aptitude is not enough: How personality and behavior predict academic performance," *J. Res. Pers.*, vol. 40, no. 3, pp. 339–346, 2006.

[19] S. Geiser and M. V. Santelices, "Validity of high-school grades in predicting student success beyond the freshman year: High school record vs. standardized tests as indicators of four-year college outcomes," *CSHE Res. Occas. Pap. Ser.*, p. 35, 2007.

[20] D. Scott, G. G. Spielmans, D. Julka, M. S. DeBerard, G. G. Spielmans, and D. Julka, "Predictors of Academic Achievement and Retention Among College Freshmen: a Longitudinal Study," *Coll. Stud. J.*, vol. 38, no. 1, pp. 66–80, 2004.

[21] M. M. Chemers, L. t Hu, and B. F. Garcia, "Academic self-efficacy and first year college student performance and adjustment," *J. Educ. Psychol.*, vol. 93, no. 1, pp. 55–64, 2001.

[22] S. B. Robbins, K. Lauver, H. Le, D. Davis, R. Langley, and A. Carlstrom, "Do psychosocial and study skill factors predict college outcomes? A meta-analysis.," *Psychol. Bull.*, vol. 130, no. 2, pp. 261–88, 2004.

[23] E. T. Pascarella and P. T. Terenzini, "Predicting freshman persistence voluntary dropout decisions from a theoretical model," *J. High. Educ.* , vol. 51, no. 1, pp. 60–75, 1980.

[24] A. W. Astin, "Student Involvement: A Developmental Theory for Higher Education Student Involvement: A Developmental Theory for Higher Education," *J. Coll. Stud. Dev.*, no. September, 1984.

[25] G. F. Ferenstein and B. J. Hershbein, "How important are high school courses to college performance? Less than you might think," *Brookings*, p. 1, 2016.

[26] E. D. Evans, D. A. McFarland, C. Rios-Aguilar, and R. Deil-Amen, "Community (in) Colleges," *Community Coll. Rev.*, vol. 44, no. 3, pp. 232–254, 2016.

[27] J. Zheng and K. Saunders, "Predictors of academic success for freshmen residence hall students.," *J. Coll. Stud. Dev.*, vol. 43, pp. 267–283, 2002.

[28] W. Camara and G. Echternacht, "The SAT-I and High School Grades: Utility in Predicting Success in College," *Res. Notes Coll. Board Off. Res. Dev.*, vol. RN-10, no. July, pp. 1–12, 2000.

[29] J. Fleming, "Who Will Succeed in College? When The SAT Predicts Black Students' Performance," *Rev. High. Educ.*, vol. 25, no. 3, pp. 281–296, 2002.

[30] J. L. Hoffman and K. E. Lowitzki, "Predicting College Success with High School Grades and Test Scores: Limitations for Minority Students," *Rev. High. Educ.*, vol. 28, no. 4, pp. 455–474, 2005.

[31] "Wolfe & Johnson (1995) - Personality as a predictor of college performance.pdf." .

[32] R. Zwick and J. C. Sklar, "Predicting College Grades and Degree Completion Using High School Grades and SAT Scores: The Role of Student Ethnicity and First Language," vol. 42, no. 3, pp. 439–464, 2005.

[33] W. Camara and M. Michaelides, "AP ® Use in Admissions: A Response to Geiser and Santelices," *Coll. Board*, pp. 1–5, 2005.

[34] M. Braxton, J, "Faculty professional choices in teaching that foster student success. tle," no. June, 2006.

[35] A. W. Astin, What matters in college?: Four critical years revisited. San Francisco: Jossey-Bass, 1993.

[36] J. G. Gaff, *General Education Today. A Critical Analysis of Controversies, Practices, and Reforms*. 433 California St., Suite 1000, San Francisco, CA 94104: Jossey-Bass, Inc., 1983.

[37] H. R. Bowen, Investment in learning: The individual and social value of American higher education (2nd ed.). New Brunswick, NJ: Transaction Publisher, 1996.

[38] W. W. Willingham, *Success in college: The role of personal qualities and academic ability*. Box 886, New York, NY 10101: College Board Publications, 1985.

[39] A. W. Astin, "Four Critical Years. Effects of College on Beliefs, Attitudes, and Knowledge," *ERIC*, 1977.

[40] G. D. Kuh, J. Kinzie, J. A. Buckley, B. K. Bridges, and J. C. Hayek, "Piecing Together the Student Success Puzzle: Research, Propositions, and Recommendations," *ASHE High. Educ. Rep.*, vol. 32, no. 5, pp. 1–182, 2007.

[41] G. D. Kuh, "What student affairs professionals need to know about student engagement," *J. Coll. Stud. Dev.*, vol. 50, no. 6, pp. 683–706, 2009.

[42] C. R. Pace, "Achievement and the Quality of Student Effort," *Natl. Comm. Excell. Educ.*, 1982.

[43] R. Junco, S. R. Cotten, P. A. Tess, P. A. Kirschner, A. C. Karpinski, and R. Junco, "Facebook?? and academic performance," *Comput. Human Behav.*, vol. 26, no. 1, pp. A60–A68, 2012.

[44] E. Moreau, "The Top 25 Social Networking Sites People Are Using," *February 13*, 2016. [Online]. Available: http://webtrends.about.com/od/socialnetworkingreviews/tp/Social-Networking-Sites.02.htm. [Accessed: 19-Feb-2017].

[45] "Top 15 Most Popular Social Networking Sites | April 2016," *Ebizmba.com*, 2016. .

[46] T. P. Alloway, J. Horton, and R. G. Alloway, "Social networking sites and cognitive abilities: Do they make you smarter?," *Comput. Educ.*, vol. 63, pp. 10–16, 2013.

[47] R. Junco, "Too much face and not enough books: The relationship between multiple indices of Facebook use and academic performance," *Comput. Human Behav.*, vol. 28, no. 1, pp. 187–198, 2012.

[48] A. B. Fox, J. Rosen, and M. Crawford, "Distractions, distractions: does instant messaging affect college students' performance on a concurrent reading comprehension task?," *CyberPsychology Behav.*, vol. 12, no. 1, pp. 51–53, 2009.

[49] D. P. Brumby and D. D. Salvucci, "Towards a Constraint Analysis of Human Multitasking," no. February, p. 2, 2006.

[50] J. P. Borst, N. A. Taatgen, and H. van Rijn, "The problem state: A cognitive bottleneck in multitasking.," *J. Exp. Psychol. Learn. Mem. Cogn.*, vol. 36, no. 2, pp. 363–382, 2010.

[51] J. P. Borst, The Problem State Bottleneck: Modeling the Behavioral and Neural Signatures of a Cognitive Bottleneck in Human Multitasking, no. September 2011. 2011.

[52] P. E. Dux, J. Ivanoff, C. L. Asplund, and R. Marois, "Isolation of a Central Bottleneck of Information Processing with Time-Resolved fMRI," *Neuron*, vol. 52, no. 6, pp. 1109–1120, 2006.

[53] "The 2015 Aspen Prize for Community College Excellence," *THE ASPEN INSTITUTE*, 2015. [Online]. Available: The 2015 Aspen Prize for Community College Excellence.

[54] R. Junco, G. Heiberger, and E. Loken, "The effect of Twitter on college student engagement and grades," *J. Comput. Assist. Learn.*, vol. 27, no. 2, pp. 119–132, 2011.

An Analysis of Security Competitions for A Beginner's Guide

Qijun Gu
qijun@txstate.edu

Tanner J. Burns
tjb102@txstate.edu

Samuel C. Rios
scr3@txstate.edu

Thomas K. Jordan
tkj15@txstate.edu

Texas State University
San Marcos, TX 78666

Trevor Underwood
tunderwood@netspend.com

Netspend Corporation
Austin, TX 78768

Abstract - Security competitions are emerging as a new approach in security education and professional training. At universities, security competitions are gradually introduced into Computer Science curriculum to attract more students into the security area and prepare them for a career in the security field. The benefits of competition-based education were recognized in many studies. However, there are still many challenges for beginners to participate in the competitions. To help beginners to study and participate, this paper analyzed thousands of competition problems in over a hundred security competitions in the past three years. This paper identifies several important characteristics of the security competitions, including the main security areas and the fundamental knowledge and skills to solve problems in these areas. This paper presents the findings as guidance to beginners so that they can find their interested areas to study and practice.

Keywords

Security Competition, Catch The Flag, Security Education, Competition Analysis, Competition Guide

1   INTRODUCTION

Over the past several years, security competitions, such as Defcon [3], CCDC [4] and many capture-the-flag (CTF) competitions [1,7,16], are emerging as a popular method of attracting promising students into security education and careers. The competitions were sponsored by either industry or government agencies and held around the United States and worldwide for high school students, college students and even professionals. They aimed to train the next generation of security professionals using hands-on competitions and to enhance the interests of a security career among the students. They have generally been seen as great methods for security education, training and recruitment.

There were many efforts to incorporate security competitions and similar practices into security education [6,8,11,13,15]. Educators and researchers have also collected empirical data to study the effectiveness of security competitions [5,14] and found that security competitions offered valuable learning experiences for computer science students as well as students in many other disciplines, such as criminology and criminal justice. The competitions improved the students' hands-on skills as well as their understandings of cyber attacks and defenses.

Although security competitions are beneficial to students interested in security, it is recognized that there are inevitable challenges for beginner students to get involved in security competitions [10,12,17]. Often, beginners got frustrated and discouraged because they were unable to solve problems. Even though they may have studied background security knowledge in class, they still lack sufficient skills in coding, networking and system administration, are not proficient in using security tools, and do not know specific security flaws. Beginners need to overcome many obstacles technically and psychologically to truly build confidence and gain benefits from the competitions.

In our experience, when beginner students were introduced to a security competition for the first time, they were often lost on what to study. Security competitions typically include a variety of security problems that need a unique set of knowledge and skills to solve. When beginners are immersed with these problems, they often do not have a clue on which problem they should start with. They are often confused by many specific security areas and cannot decide which areas best match their interests and strengths.

To help beginners gain confidence and start participating in competitions, the main goal of this paper is to give a clear picture to beginners that shows (1) the main security areas in competitions, (2) the main characteristics of competitions and competition problems, and (3) the main security knowledge and skill sets necessary to solve some common problems. With this guidance, beginners can choose specific subjects to study and prepare in order to become capable of solving a few problems in their initial attempts.

The contribution of this paper is established on a comprehensive study and analysis of over 3000 competition problems used in 160 security competitions held during 2014 to 2016. To our best knowledge, this is the first study to collect, analyze and characterize a vast amount of problems of past competitions. After analysis, we summarized the nature of the security competitions in recent years, identified six common security problem categories, and identified the mostly used knowledge and skill sets in the security areas. With these findings, we thus make our beginner's guide that recommends some must-have skill sets for beginners to study.

In the rest of the paper, we first describe our methods of collecting and analyzing data in Section 2. We present the main characteristics of the security problems in Section 3. Then, we present guidance for beginners to study in Section 4. Finally, we discuss the related work on using security competitions in computer science education in Section 5 and conclude in Section 6.

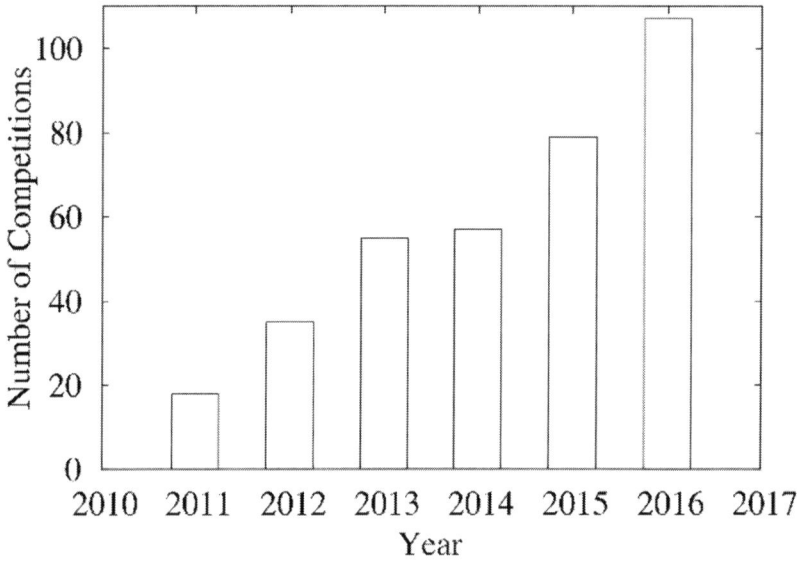

(a) Number of Competitions Over Years

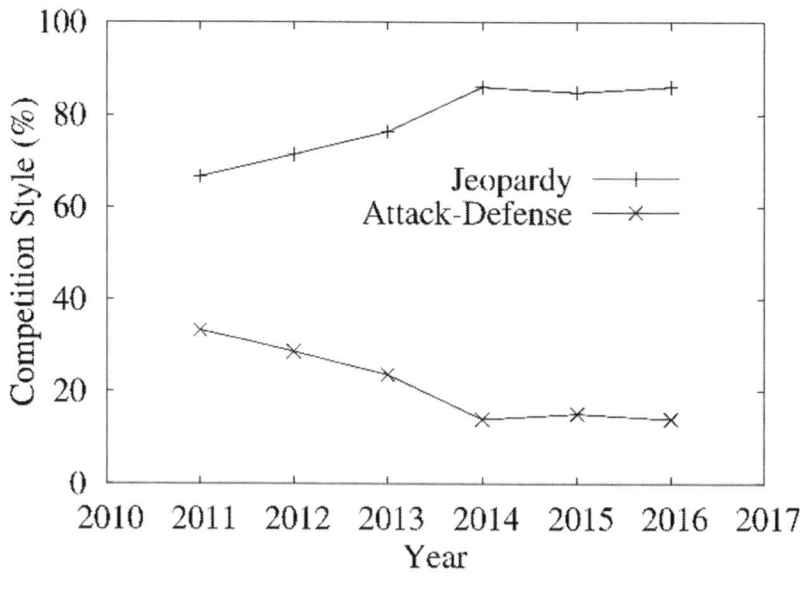

(b) Competition Styles

Figure 1: Characteristics of Past Competitions

2 DATA COLLECTION AND ANALYSIS OF COMPETITIONS

2.1 Security Competitions

Many security competitions have taken place around the world in recent years. We collected the data of the past competitions during 2011 and 2016 from the archives of CTFtime.org [1]. Figure 1(a) shows that the number of competitions had linear growth in the past six years. Security competitions have clearly been attracting more and more hosts and players in industry and academy for not only training security professionals but also business–involved activities, such as recruiting, advertising and so on.

Security competitions are often categorized as jeopardy style, where players use offensive techniques to solve security problems, defense style, where players need to defend their vulnerable services, and attack- defense style, where players need to take both offensive and defensive actions against other players. We analyzed the competition styles based on the data from CTFtime.org. We noticed that the data only has the jeopardy style and the attack-defense style competitions, and does not include any defense-only competitions. Figure 1(b) shows that more jeopardy style competitions were emerging in the past years. The numbers of the attack-defense style competitions were stable in the range of six to thirteen every year.

2.2 Security Problems and Categories

To better understand the types of competition problems and the associated skills that are required to solve them, we collected and analyzed not only security problems but also their solutions. Many players voluntarily posted their solutions as "writeups" that provide step-by-step solutions with commentary about their thought processes. The writeups are excellent resources for beginners to study and follow. Beginners can find the writeups on Github [2], CTFtime [1], players' personal blogs or websites, and so on. After comparing these sources, we chose to collect writeups from Github [2] due to the larger quantity and better quality of the submitted writeups. For many problems, we found multiple writeups to compare their solutions.

We collected and analyzed the writeups posted for security competitions in 2014, 2015 and 2016. There were very limited writeups before 2014 on Github, and they were scattered over other sources. In total, we collected 3598 security problems of 160 security competitions. Because the writeups are completely volunteer-based, not all security competitions have writeups. The collected writeups cover 34 of 57 (60%) security competitions in 2014, 56 of 79 (71%) security competitions in 2015, and 70 of 107 (65%) security competitions in 2016. We noticed that there are missing security problems across the 160 competitions. We could not verify how many problems are missing because we could not obtain the original problems from many past competitions.

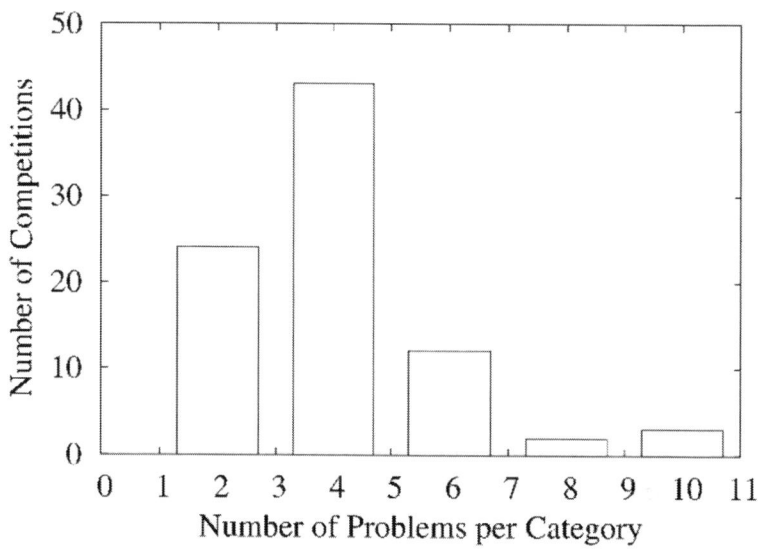

(a) Histogram of Problem Counts

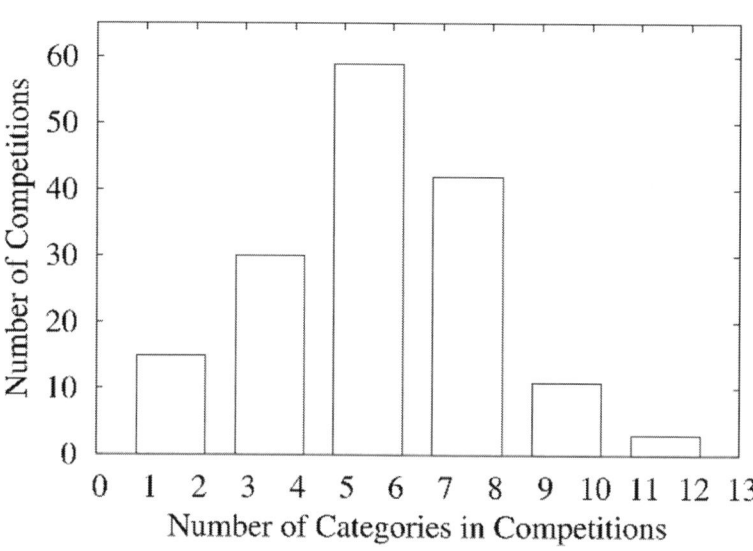

(b) Histogram of Category Counts

Figure 2: Characteristics of Problems and Categories

Figure 2(a) shows the histogram of the number of security problems with corresponding writeups on Github. Most competitions have about 20 or 30 security problems. Ten competitions have fewer than five problems with writeups. Upon further inspection, we found that two of the ten competitions were teaser competitions that did not have many problems. Two were for high school students that maybe did not have enough players to provide writeups. Two were some sort of easy qualification competitions. The remaining four might not have had enough players.

Most security competitions divided their security problems into a variety of categories. Similar problems were grouped in the same category. However, the competitions did not always name the categories in the same way. We analyzed the 909 category names used in the 160 competitions. To avoid duplication, we combined similar category names. For example, the categories "pwn", "pwnable" and "pwning" were combined to "pwn". Then, we reduced them to 77 unique category names in these competitions. We found six top category names: "crypto", "web", "reverse", "forensic", "pwn" and "misc". They represent the major categories of security problems and security areas in competitions. Often, the problems of the other categories overlap with the six categories. For example, the problems of "exploit" often belong to either "pwn" or "web", and the problems of "binary" often belong to either "reverse" or "pwn".

To make our analysis more concise and useful to beginners, we kept the six categories. We read and analyzed the writeups of the problems of the other categories and reclassified them to the six categories based on the key goals of the problems. For example, some "stegano" and "recon" problems are to extract hidden or obfuscated information, and thus are re-classified to the "forensic" category. "ppc" and "trivia" problems are reclassified to the "misc" category because they do not actually address security issues. Some original "misc" problems were reclassified to the other categories because they addressed some sort of security issues.

Categories	Problems	Reclassification
Crypto	Cryptographic problems	crypto, web, network
Web	Web exploitation problems	web, exploit, recon, network, misc
Reverse	Reverse engineering problems	reverse, binary, misc
Forensic	Data extraction problems	forensic, stegano, recon, network, misc
Pwn	Exploit remote services	pwn, exploit, network, binary, misc
Misc	Coding and non-security problems	misc, trivia, ppc

Table 1: Categories and Reclassification

Table 1 shows the six categories used in this paper and the reclassification of the categories used in the collected competitions. With fewer categories, our analysis provides more focused sets of security knowledge, skills and techniques for beginners to study.

3   ANALYSIS OF COMPETITION PROBLEMS

In this study, we read the security problems and the corresponding writeups. We discussed together the problems and the solutions from the writeups every week. The weekly discussion made us stay on a common ground for analyzing the problems and solutions. While studying the problems, we recorded the characteristics of the problems and tested the methods and tools of the solutions.

After reading all writeups of the collected 3598 problems, we further excluded 1400 problems from our analysis because their writeups are actually missing or do not have complete solutions. We then analyzed the remaining 2198 problems that have good writeups to identify and summarize the information that can help beginners to study and prepare for security competitions.

3.1 Difficulty Levels

A security competition usually assigns different points to the security problems to indicate their difficulty levels. The greater the point, the more difficult a problem is. Because each competition targets different kinds of players, there is no common criteria among the competitions to evaluate difficulty levels of the security problems. For example, some easy problems in Defcon's qualification competitions were equivalent to hard problems in competitions for high school students. Furthermore, there is no common approach to assign points to the security problems. Some competitions assigned two-digit points while others assigned three-digit or four-digit points.

Even though security problems vary, after reading many writeups, we observed that players need to possess specific technical skills, identify key methods of the problems, and use a few tools in order to solve the problems. Therefore, we define three difficulty levels below with a mixed qualitative and quantitative approach that bases the levels on the key components of the solutions from the perspectives of beginners. Referring to the points that were assigned to the problems, we re-evaluated the problems and assigned the three difficulty levels to them. We can then more fairly identify the basic and advanced skills for beginners to learn.

1. *Easy*: A problem can be solved with one or two methods and tools. A beginner can often solve the problem by themselves right after reading the writeups.

2. *Medium*: A problem can be solved with three or more methods and tools. After reading the writeups, a beginner can solve the problem with extra efforts, such as reading additional documents.

3. *Hard*: A problem can be solved with in-depth methods and sophisticated tools. A beginner can hardly understand the writeups and cannot solve the problem even after reading the writeups.

In total, more than a third of problems are easy ones. With proper studying and preparations, beginners can solve many of these easy problems in competitions and gain confidence and successful experiences. With such seed encouragement, they may gain more motivations to further their study in security.

3.2 Problem Characteristics

Based on the writeups, we identified three main characteristics of competition problems: (1) coding languages for pwn, web, reverse and misc, (2) cryptographic algorithms for crypto, and (3) data types for forensic. These characteristics reflect the minimum essential knowledge and skills that are required to solve the easy problems. These characteristics are category-specific. For example, coding language is a key characteristic of the problems in the "pwn", "web", "reverse" and "misc" categories, because players must understand the coding languages of the problems in these four categories in order to solve the problems. Coding languages are not essential for solving "crypto" or "forensic" problems, because "crypto" problems require players to understand cryptography and "forensic" problems require players to be familiar with various data types and formats.

3.2.1 Coding Languages

In many security problems, a set of programs were provided to players. The players needed to read and understand the programs and then find the key information (such as flaws) in the programs to solve the problems. Because these programs were made in a variety of coding languages, typical challenges for beginners are (i) what coding languages they need to learn and (ii) how to quickly understand a program coded in a language they do not know. We analyzed the data pertaining to coding languages to find some suggestions for the first challenge below. For the second challenge, we think that if beginners can master a few mostly used coding languages in competitions, they can "guess" the programs in other coding languages to some extent.

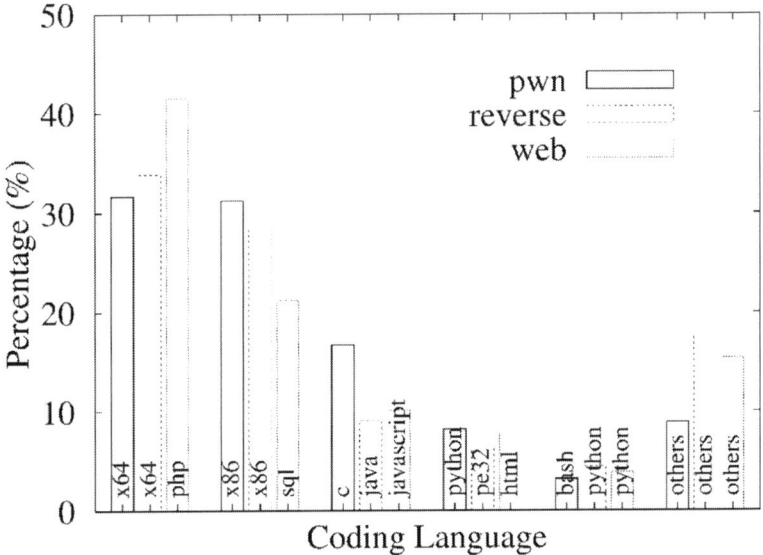

Figure 3: Coding Languages

Figure 3 shows the percentage breakdown of the coding languages in the "pwn", "reverse" and "web" categories. Only the top 5 languages of each category are listed.

In the "pwn" category, the top two coding languages are x64 assembly and x86 assembly that are used in executable binaries. Players are often required to disassemble and decompile provided binaries to find flaws and then solve the problems. When binaries were not provided in competitions, a portion of source files that built the remote services were provided to players. Then, players discovered the flaws in the provided source code to solve the problems. C and Python are the top two coding language used to build the remote services in competitions. Bash is among the top five because it is a system administration language widely used in Unix and Linux computers. Compared with "reverse" and "web", the top five languages are dominant in the "pwn" category. Only 16 other programming languages were occasionally used in the "pwn" problems.

The "reverse" category has the same top two languages as "pwn", since most "reverse" problems were to reverse engineer executable ELF-based Linux binaries. Meanwhile, there are many other types of executable programs too. Java ranks third, because many problems asked players to analyze Java programs and Android applications that can both be decompiled to Java language. PE32 is a type of executable binaries running in Windows computers and ranks fourth. Because many competitions were hosted on Linux computers, PE32 binaries were not as popular as x64 and x86 binaries. Python programs are becoming popular too, and python bytecode was often used in the "reverse" problems. In total, we identified 26 other programming languages with lower ranks in the "reverse" category. They were mostly for specific programs, such as mobile devices (such as ARM) or game machines (such as Nintendo).

The top 2 languages in the "web" category are used on the server side. PHP-based web applications were mostly exploited through some well-known PHP's flaws in competitions. In addition, LAMP (Linux, Apache, Mysql and PHP) is a very common web framework. Many websites in competitions were setup based on this framework. Hence, PHP is the number one language in the "web" category. Because web sites are often backed with SQL databases, SQL ranks 2nd. In particular, most SQL databases were Mysql database in competitions. Javascript and HTML are the languages used on the client side and rank 3rd and 4th. But, because Node.js is emerging as a new server-side web development framework, some Javascript problems were on the security issues in Node.js. Python and Perl (not shown in the figure) rank 5th and 6th respectively, as they are also popular web development language. 21 other programming languages on either the server-side or client-side were used in the web exploitation problems.

3.2.2   Cryptographic Algorithms

A variety of cryptographic algorithms were used in the "crypto" problems. Not counting custom algorithms, we identified 45 publicly known cryptographic algorithms. Figure 4 shows the percentage breakdown of the problems based on these cryptographic algorithms and listed those that appeared in more than 1% of problems. More than a third of "crypto" problems used custom cryptographic algorithms. For these problems, the competition hosts generally provided the source code files that contain the algorithms. Players needed to find flaws in the algorithms to solve the problems. The remaining publicly known cryptographic algorithms include almost all major algorithms nowadays. Some of the algorithms have well known flaws and the others were used in a flawed way in competitions. Symmetric cryptographic algorithms appeared in about a third of problems. We identified 36 publicly known symmetric algorithms, much more than the counts of the other kinds of publicly known cryptographic algorithms. Asymmetric cryptographic algorithms appeared in about a fifth of problems, but has only ten algorithms. Among all publicly known cryptographic algorithms, RSA was the mostly used in competitions. Hash algorithms appeared in about 5.3% of problems. MD5 has well known collision issues and thus appeared in more problems than SHA1 and SHA2. The "misc" group includes the problems that were designed based on cryptographic tools, libraries and protocols.

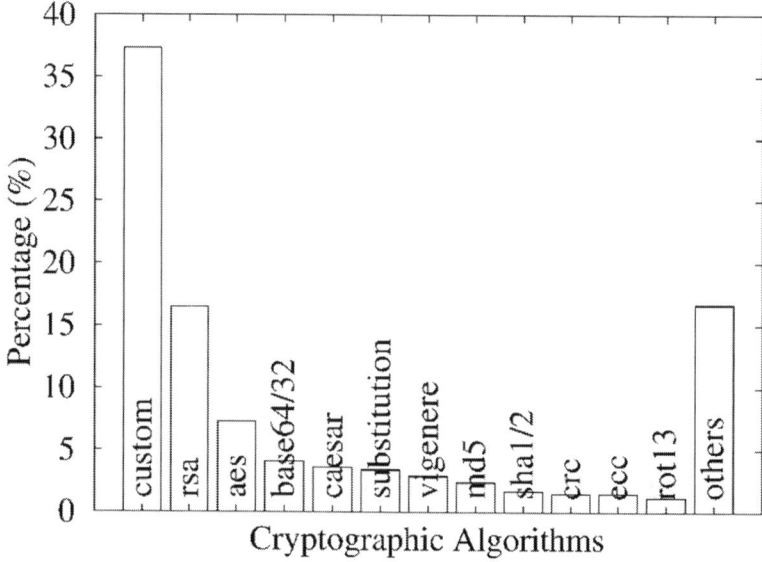

Figure 4: Cryptographic Algorithms

3.2.3 Data Types

The main objectives of problems in the "forensic" category are to extract information from various types of data files. Often, steganographic methods as well as cryptographic approaches were used together to hide information in provided data files. Among the collected problems, we identified 69 unique file formats used in the problems and divided them to 16 data types. Figure 5 shows the percentages of the problems of the top 10 data types.

Images are the number one data type, and PNG and JPG are the top two image formats. Many forensic problems embedded data in the meta information of images, concatenating multiple image files, tweaking image pixels and so on. The second most common challenges were analyzing PCAP and TCPCUMP network trace files. Players needed to follow the network traffic in the traces to find the information. The third is multimedia data, including audio, video and streaming. Information was usually hidden as a secondary track or encoded in the time or frequency domains of the multimedia data. The other data types appeared in about one third of problems and all have their unique methods to hide information.

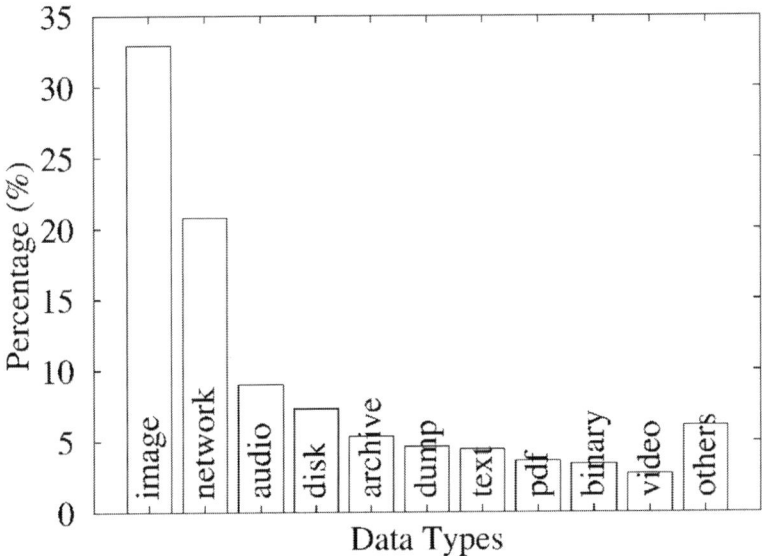

Figure 5: Data Types

4   GUIDE FOR BEGINNERS

Our analysis shows the main characteristics of competition problems. We think these characteristics not only reflect the main security issues concerned by industry and academy, but also deliver clearly to beginners what they need to study and practice for participating in security competitions. In the following, we recommend the most common knowledge and skill sets we found in our analysis as a guide for beginners. The goal of this guide is to identify many specific essential skills that are very often needed in competitions. Thereby, after learning the outlined skill sets, beginners can solve at least some easy problems in competitions. In short, beginners need to be very proficient in programming and analytics. Without the proficiency in these two skill sets, beginners cannot solve even easy problems in a timely manner.

4.1 Programming

Python appears to be the dominant programming language in the solutions of many competition problems. It is easy for beginners to learn and begin using. Beginners can quickly make some python scripts and run them to test solutions. There are a lot of supporting libraries to handle networking, web, strings, numbers, arithmetic, and various files in Python.

There are two main programming skill sets that beginners must be proficient with. The first is number, string and file manipulations, such as hexadecimal and binary conversions, string and number conversions, large number arithmetic, base64 encoding and decoding, string splitting and concatenation, and so on. Many problems provide files for analysis. Beginners should be able to open, read and analyze files in a programmable way. The second is network programming that is required to interact with remote servers in many competitions problems. Beginners shall be able to do socket programming, preferably with some well-known libraries, such as pwnlib. Thereby, beginners are able to create services, make and send arbitrary packets to remote servers, and process packets sent from remote servers. To assist with network programming, beginners should be proficient with common networking tools, such as netstat, netcat and so on.

4.2 Analytics

Analytics are mostly category-specific. In the following, we summarize the major analytic techniques according to the five security categories in Table 1 (excluding the "misc" category). Beginners are not expected to learn absolutely everything that is incorporated into all of the competitions. Rather, they should focus on what they are interested in and develop the skill sets accordingly.

Reverse: As discussed in Section 3.2.1, players often need to disassemble and decompile the executable programs in x64, x86 or Java bytecode to find flaws and then solve the problems. The executable programs are usually decompiled to source code in C or Java. Hence, beginners need to understand four coding languages: x64 assemly, x86 assembly, C and Java. In addition, beginners need to proficiently use hex tools, disassemblers and decompilers, such as Hexdump, GDB, Hopper and IDA Pro, so that they can figure out the programming logic in the binaries.

Pwn: The problems of this categories usually requires reverse engineering to enumerate the target. Hence, in addition to the analytic techniques of the "reverse" category, beginners need to study how to exploit flaws in remote servers. Typical exploitable flaws include buffer overflow, heap overflow, format string, returnoriented programming, etc. Beginners also need to study how to make exploiting packets that exploit the flaws to attack and control the remote servers with network programming. Because the problems of the "pwn" category require more techniques, they are typically harder than the problems in the other categories. Beginners should consider "pwn" as an advanced level to "reverse".

Web: The web problems require knowledge of web technologies on both server side and client side. On the server side, beginners should familiarize themselves with PHP language, SQL language, and MySQL database, and then understand how to launch SQL injection attacks. On the client side, beginners need to study Javascript and HTML to understand how web pages are dynamically generated and rendered on the client side. Furthermore, beginners should be proficient with the use of CURL and web development tools built in most web browsers to inspect web pages and web traffics. Beginners need to inspect and manipulate cookies, sessions, URLs, form data, JSON data and web agents on the client side.

Crypto: Based on Figure 4, beginners need to master a few cryptographic algorithms. For asymmetric cryptography, beginners need to make RSA encryption and decryption programs or use exiting RSA tools and libraries. Beginners also need to study and be able to exploit a few common RSA implementation flaws, such as weak public keys and Coppersmith's attack. For symmetric cryptography, beginners need to study AES-ECB encryption and crack it when it is used in an insecure manner. Usually, easy crypto problems were based on Caesar cipher, substitution cipher, Vigenere cipher, and XOR operators. Hence, beginners should study them. In hash, beginners need to study how to perform hash reverse lookup and conduct length extension attacks on MD5 and SHA1.

Forensic: For the problems of this category, beginners mainly need to know the file formats: file signatures, file structures, file headers, file meta information and so on. As discussed in Section 3.2.3, there are a few file types often used in these problems, including PNG, JPEG, PCAP, WAV, AVI, Disk dump, and ZIP. Once beginners are familiar with the formats of these major file types, they will be able to detect hidden information in the files or repair the corrupted files.

5   RELATED WORKS

In recent years, security competitions have been gradually incorporated into the Computer Science education in more and more universities [6,8,9,11,13,14,18]. Despite these efforts and recognized advantages of these new security education approaches, educators and researchers have recognized several issues of security competitions that are particularly challenging to beginners. In [10], six factors were presented to analyze the reasons that security competitions were often very hard to beginners. Among the six factors, three factors were on the design process of competition problems. It was argued that most security problems were designed on heavy technical requirements, some were made harder with artificially added constraints, and many were developed without a proper quality assurance process. For these reasons, the competition problems were not designed for beginners in the first place, and thus led to beginners quickly becoming stuck and giving up.

Additional studies have been conducted to attempt to engage beginners. In [12], a set of small-scoped and hands-on exercises in defense and offense were designed for class use. The goal was to gently introduce beginners to security competitions, rather than simply exposing them to hard problems that they cannot solve. After the exercises, the teacher led an in-class analysis that provided the critical feedback and enabled students to identify the achievements and the areas that require additional practices. In [17], another effort was developed to help beginners. In the study, security problems were divided into several levels. Each level provided a few hints as well as a recommended solution as a last resort. Players could opt to take the hints and the solutions. However, the study did not find a convincing evidence that players were positively benefited from the hints and the solutions. In this research, we were also concerned on beginners. Our research was focused on helping beginners understand the characteristics of the security competitions and the competition problems so that beginners know what areas and what skills they need to learn in order to participate in the competitions.

6   CONCLUSION

During the course of this paper, we analyzed 160 security competitions taking place during 2014 and 2016 and over 3000 problems in these competitions. The goal of this analysis is to provide a clear picture of the main characteristics of security competitions to beginners. This analysis shows that, with a growing number of security competitions every year, online jeopardy style competitions are the main form of competitions for beginners to participate. There are six dominant categories of problems in these competitions. Each category represents a security area that requires a unique set of knowledge and technical skills, including programming languages, data and file types, and cryptographic algorithms. Therefore, we recommend a few fundamental techniques beginners should study for each category. Currently, we are building a platform with a set of exercises that incorporate the knowledge and skills. We will test the platform in our classes to engage more students in security competitions.

REFERENCES

[1] CTF Time. https://ctftime.org/.

[2] CTF Write-ups. https://github.com/ctfs.

[3] DEF CON Hacking Conference. https://www.defcon.org/.

[4] National Collegiate Cyber Defense Competition. http://www.nationalccdc.org/.

[5] Masooda Bashir, April Lambert, Jian Ming Colin Wee, and Boyi Guo. An Examination of the Vocational and Psychological Characteristics of Cybersecurity Competition Participants. In Proc. of USENIX Summit on Gaming, Games, and Gamification in Security Education, 2015.

[6] Martin Carlisle, Michael Chiaramonte, and David Caswell. Using CTFs for an Undergraduate Cyber Education. In Proc. of USENIX Summit on Gaming, Games, and Gamification in Security Education, August 2015.

[7] Peter Chapman, Jonathan Burket, and David Brumley. PicoCTF: A Game-Based Computer Security Competition for High School Students. In Proc. of USENIX Summit on Gaming, Games, and Gamifi- cation in Security Education, August 2014.

[8] Tom Chothia and Chris Novakovic. An Offline Capture The Flag-Style Virtual Machine and an Assessment of Its Value for Cybersecurity Education. In Proc. USENIX Summit on Gaming, Games, and Gamification in Security Education, 2015.

[9] Tom Chothia and Joeri de Ruiter. Learning From Others' Mistakes: Penetration Testing IoT Devices in the Classroom. In Proc. of USENIX Workshop on Advances in Security Education, 2016.

[10] Kevin Chung and Julian Cohen. Learning Obstacles in the Capture The Flag Model. In Proc. of USENIX Summit on Gaming, Games, and Gamification in Security Education, August 2014.

[11] Adrian Dabrowski, Markus Kammerstetter, Eduard Thamm, Edgar Weippl, and Wolfgang Kastner. Leveraging Competitive Gamification for Sustainable Fun and Profit in Security Education. In Proc. of USENIX Summit on Gaming, Games, and Gamification in Security Education, 2015.

[12] Jelena Mirkovic, Aimee Tabor, Simon Woo, and Portia Pusey. Engaging Novices in Cybersecurity Competitions: A Vision and Lessons Learned at ACM Tapia

2015. In Proc. of USENIX Summit on Gaming, Games, and Gamification in Security Education, 2015.

[13] W. Michael Petullo, Kyle Moses, Ben Klimkowski, Ryan Hand, and Karl Olson. The Use of Cyber- Defense Exercises in Undergraduate Computing Education. In Proc. of USENIX Workshop on Ad- vances in Security Education, 2016.

[14] Aunshul Rege. Multidisciplinary Experiential Learning for Holistic Cybersecurity Education, Research and Evaluation. In Proc. of USENIX Summit on Gaming, Games, and Gamification in Security Education, 2015.

[15] Z. Cliffe Schreuders and Emlyn Butterfield. Gamification for Teaching and Learning Computer Security in Higher Education. In Proc. of USENIX Workshop on Advances in Security Education, 2016.

[16] Giovanni Vigna, Kevin Borgolte, Jacopo Corbetta, Adam Doup´e, Yanick Fratantonio, Luca Invernizzi, Dhilung Kirat, and Yan Shoshitaishvili. Ten Years of iCTF: The Good, The Bad, and The Ugly. In Proc. of USENIX Summit on Gaming, Games, and Gamification in Security Education, 2014.

[17] Jan Vykopal and Milo˘s Bart˘ak. On the Design of Security Games: From Frustrating to Engaging Learning. In Proc. of USENIX Workshop on Advances in Security Education, 2016.

[18] Chuan Yue. Teaching Computer Science With Cybersecurity Education Built- in. In Proc. of USENIX Workshop on Advances in Security Education, 2016.

Applying Nodal Governance to Combat Cybercrime: An Novel Approach

Charles Wilson
wilsonce@udmercy.edu

Gregory Laidlaw
laidlags@udmercy.edu

University of Detroit Mercy
Center for Cyber Security and Intelligence Studies

Abstract - This paper will address the impact of the ever-increasing phenomenon of cybercrime in America. It will argue that cybercrime as a new genre of illegal behavior (criminality) is having a significantly negative impact on key aspects of America's national security, financial prosperity, and public safety. The premise of the paper is that the contemporary cyberthreat landscape is an evolving target surface with a growing cast of nation-states, transnational organized criminal organizations, and other criminal actors who are continually changing and updating their modus operandi to maintain an advantage over cybersecurity defenders. Moreover, as cybercrime incidents increase in frequency, harm, danger, and cost, the cybersecurity programs of public and private sector defenders may be incapable of effectively countering the threat, and the resulting growth in scale of cybercrime will continue to challenge and possibly overwhelm the capabilities of the federal-centric national cybersecurity strategy currently employed to counter this threat. The increasing and invasive nature of cybercrime mandates a critical and urgent need for enhanced capabilities and increased levels of expertise in combating, preventing, investigating, and policing cybercrime incidents. This paper recommends that American policymakers continue to recognize the level of threat presented by this damaging and noxious form of crime and in response adopt policies that foster implementation of an overarching national cybersecurity strategy based on the nodal governance of security. The paper recommendations that the U.S. government create operational policies and funding provisions to include and maximize the use of civil sector's capabilities and enhance law enforcement capabilities by expanding the use of local, state, and county police agencies in the campaign against cybercrime.

Keywords

cybercrime, cybersecurity, cyberthreat, nodal governance

1 INTRODUCTION

This paper will examine the issue of cybercrime and its impact on critical aspects of American national security, economic prosperity, cybersecurity, public safety, and the lives of its citizens. The paper recommends that the U.S. government create operational policies and funding provisions to include and maximize the use of civil sector's capabilities and enhance law enforcement capabilities by expanding the use of local, state, and county police agencies in the campaign against cybercrime. This is a process called "capacity development (CD)" which is recognized in the literature as the creation of national capacity and is described as more than state-centric capacity. The CD process must recognize that the civil sector comprised of non-state actors have a legitimate role to play in the capacity development process and therefore should be part of any national CD process. It also means that our understanding of security governance needs to be one that recognizes the participation of the civil sector entities as key stakeholders, especially in cyberspace governance and cybersecurity.

The United Nations (UN) was one of the first global governance organization to recognize and conceptualize capacity development. The United Nations Secretariat defines capacity development as "the process by which people, organizations and society systematically stimulate and develop their capability over time to achieve social and economic goals, through the accession of improved of knowledge, skills, systems, and institutions – within a wider social and cultural enabling environment." The term evolved to be "community capacity building" which defines capacity building as a long-term continual process of development that involves all stakeholders; including ministries, local authorities, non-governmental organizations, professionals, community members, academics and more. Capacity development uses a country's human, scientific, technological, organizational, and institutional and resource capabilities. The goal of capacity development is to resolve problems related to policy and methods of development, while considering the potential, limits and needs of the people of the country concerned. Capacity development takes place on an individual level, an institutional level and the societal level.

- Individual level – it requires the development of conditions that allow individual stakeholders to build and enhance knowledge, skills and abilities. It also calls for the establishment of conditions that will allow individuals to engage in the "process of learning and adapting to change.

- Institutional level – it should involve enabling existing institutions and providing the necessary support in the form of sound policies, organizational structures, and effective methods of management and revenue streams.

- Societal level – it should support the establishment of a more "interactive public administration that learns equally from its actions and from feedback it receives from the population at large." Community capacity building must be used to develop public administrators that are responsive and accountable. The computer as a target—attacking the computers of others (e.g. spreading viruses).

This paper will survey the topic through an extensive literature review and provide an in-formative summary of what the empirical literature presents as evidence of the rising menace of cybercrime. The Department of Justice categorizes computer crime, also called cybercrime, in three ways:

1. The computer as a target—attacking the computers of others (e.g. spreading viruses).

2. The computer as a weapon—using a computer to commit "traditional crime" that we see in the physical world (e.g. fraud or illegal gambling).

3. The computer as an accessory—using a computer as a "fancy filing cabinet" to store illegal or stolen information.

Moreover, the literature clearly demonstrates that cybercrime is a far more serious threat to the U.S. than many other nations, because the U.S. national security, economy, and critical infrastructure are far more dependent and operated through cyber systems than most other nations. Furthermore, there are no restrictions or limitations on the selection of a cybercrime target, as noted by Lior Kohavi (2015):

Cybercrime is, at its heart, a business and as with any other business, it runs on profits .... cybercrime gangs have evolved into sophisticated operation; they perform market research to understand their most lucrative market segments, use in-house or outsourced development teams to build new "product" ... to drive threat penetration, and they use a complex network of distribution partners for threat delivery. (p. 1)

2 THE SCOPE AND SCALE OF CYBERCRIME THREAT

There is no current and official source to accurately determine the true cost of cybercrime in America. McAfee (2014) estimated that the global economic impact of cybercrime was annually more than $400 billion. In America, the Federal Bureau of Investigation's (FBI) Internet Crime Complaint Center (IC3) tallied 269,422 complaints in 2014, totaling $800,492,073 in losses; and the center received 3,175,611 complaints since its establishment in May 2000. These estimated totals are much lower than actual cybercrime losses. The IC3 report states, "Only an estimated 15 percent of the nation's fraud victims report their crimes to law enforcement, while the IC3 estimates less than 10 percent of victims file directly through the IC3.gov. website" (p. 6). A Ponemon Institute (2014) revealed that the average cost of cybercrime for U.S. retail stores more than doubled in 2013 to an annual average of $8.6 million per company. The annual average cost per company of successful cyberattacks increased to $20.8 million in financial services, $14.5 million in the technology sector, and $12.7 million in communications industries. The cost of cybercrime also should be expanded to include the more than 40 million individual U.S. citizens who suffer by having their personal identity stolen (McAfee, 2014).

The reviewed literature illustrates that America's growing dependence on technology will continue to provide a target-rich environment for the rising trend of cybercrime because information technology is used in virtually every aspect of contemporary life. According to Internet World Stats (2016) the level of Internet penetration in the U.S. is very high, with Internet users using online services to transact purchases and/or pay for merchandise via credit/debit cards linked to their banking accounts at a rate of 89.3%, ranking 1st in the world. Additionally, the U.S. is currently the largest economy in the world, which makes it the number one target for cybercriminals. The persistent increases in the frequency and severity of cyberattacks on U.S. targets show a clear threat to public and private sector entities, and individual citizens; with ominous implications for undermining U.S. institutions in the areas of national security, financial system, and public safety.

Today, the global internet population is estimated to consist of over 3.2 billion individuals (Murphy & Roser, 2017). The number of Internet-connected devices is predicted to grow fivefold by 2020, the number of connected devices growing to over 50 billion (Evans, 2012). In America, approximately 286 million individuals or 9 of every 10 American adults (89.3%) use the internet (Pew Research, 2017). By any measure, the U.S. is a prime target and fertile hunting ground for cybercriminals looking for a major score in cyberspace. Factors such as the economic level of a country, its Internet population, and the security level of the nation coalesce to define a geography of attacks (Paganini, 2012). For cybercriminals, the U.S. represents the perfect attack surface.

The perfect attack surface is comprised of a target rich environment consisting of opportunities for cybercriminals to attack victims in the public, private, and civil sectors. It should be noted and emphasized that this paper is making special note of the civil sector because that sector of American society is often overlooked and/or totally ignored in the extant literature and national policy deliberation processes related to cybersecurity. The civil sector is described and understood as:

> **Civil society** is the "aggregate of non-governmental organizations and institutions that manifest interests and will of citizens". Civil society includes the family and the private sphere, referred to as the "third sector" of society, distinct from government and business (Dictionary.com, 21st Century Lexicon).

Other literature has noted that the civil sector is the aggregation of non-governmental organizations, collective civic groups and social institutions that manifest shared interests and the will of citizens, individuals and organizations in a society. The civil sector is independent of the public (government) and private business) sectors, however, it is the catalytic agent that energizes the public and private sectors' activity in such a way as to strengthen the common good (World Economic Forum, 2013). The confluence of globalization, the Internet, and increasing rates of information exchange and technological transfer are having a significant influence on shaping global governance processes. The civil sector is playing an ever-increasing and important role in the global governance arena by creating social capital and driving policy change through what has been described as a global associational revolution. This revolution is described as a focused mobilization of organized civil sector organizations, engaging in voluntary activity across the geopolitical and socioeconomic dimensions of the world (Salamon, et al., 1999.). The revolutionary entities are comprised of an assemblage of independent and distinct civic associations, social networks, commonwealth organizations and normative groups, based on common interests, mutual trust and shared benefits that enable groups and individuals to cooperate with one another for the common good.

The rising menace of cybercrime is rapidly becoming a major concern for cybersecurity defenders who are responsible for implementing measures that will be most effective in preventing, reducing, or mitigating the threats to computers, network systems, and any other connected devices or critical infrastructures. A retrospective examination of the number, scale and cost of cybercrime episodes illustrate that both have continued to grow at an exponential rate. For example, Security Intelligence (Kassem, 2016) stated that during 2015 cybercrime was a crime epidemic of a magnitude and sophistication that will only continue to accelerate, intensify and increase to exponential proportions in the future. The literature clearly illustrate that organized crime, transnational criminal organizations, and affiliated black-hat hackers are forming criminal networks, and have become significantly more brazen, bold and persistent in their modus operandi. Cyber criminals will continually upgrade their techniques to incorporate the very latest emerging technology into their cybercrime activities (Goodman, 2015). According to a 2014 study of the criminal groups operating in cyberspace, a full 80% of hackers are now working with or are active co-conspirators in organized criminal organizations perpetrating in cyberspace (Broadhurst, et. al., 2014). The economic damage caused by cybercrime is extremely huge and assessable. According Sameer Dixit, Senior director of Security at cybersecurity firm Spirent, in 2016 both individuals, businesses, and government agencies were struck by 90 million cyberattacks (Broadhurst, et al. 2014). The American civil sector has multiple and diverse capabilities, expertise, and skills which should be tapped by the U.S. Government as a functional enhancement to improve the overall effort in preventing, countering and responding to cybercrime attacks. According to Ghaus-Pasha (2004):

Civil society has been widely recognized as an essential 'third' sector. Its strength can have a positive influence on the state and the market. Civil society is therefore seen as an increasingly important agent for promoting good governance like transparency, effectiveness, openness, responsiveness and accountability (p. 3).

3   NODAL GOVERNANCE OF SECURITY - A STRATEGIC CONCEPT FOR COMBATING CYBERCRIME

As the U.S. strives to come to terms with the increasing threat of cybercrime, the country's political leaders, policy makers, and business executives must begin to develop and implement the right policies, laws, and strategies needed to effectively address this challenge. This paper proposes that the nodal governance of security is the appropriate strategic concept most capable of effectively answering the challenges presented by cybercrime; this paper, also, recommends that polycentric security and policing be employed as the operational and tactical framework for implementing cybercrime counter measures. Together, both concepts can be crafted and fused into an integrated approach for improving cybersecurity focused on the prevention, mitigation, and response to cybercrime. In the form of an integrated and unified strategic approach to combating cybercrime, nodal governance of security and polycentric policing offer a method for mobilizing all available resources, expertise, and capabilities.

In the development and launch of any concept of cybersecurity intended for the purpose of countering cybercrime, it is critical to harness the power and capabilities of all stakeholders, especially the private and civil sectors. Cybercriminals are equal-opportunities perpetrators, meaning they will target and attack any victim that will quickly and profitably make them money (Kohavi, 2015). In a cyber environment with ever-changing risks and threats, the government needs to do more to support the private and civil sectors, and local law enforcement in establishing robust support for cybercrime counter-measures while not creating regulations that hinder the operational freedom of those most responsible for security and policing cyberspace.

3.1 IAD-SES Framework

Professor Elinor Ostrom created an informative framework of eight design principles for the management of common-pool resources known as the Institutional Analysis and Design (IAD). The framework that she proposes can be used as a basis for collaboration and a more robust cooperative resource-sharing arrangement between the parties actively working to reduce cybercrime. By proposing a framework for sharing information and resources, it is hoped that enforcement efforts can be handled by the nodes with the needed skill, duplications of effort can be eliminated, and crimes that are not currently investigated due to lack of expertise or geographic dispersion can be given proper attention. The rules proposed by Professor Ostrom are designed to facilitate information and resource sharing between organizations, and are as follows:

1. "clearly defined boundaries for the user pool and the resource domain"

2. "proportional equivalence between benefits and costs"

3. "collective choice arrangements [ensuring] that the resource users participate in setting... rules"

4. "monitoring...by the appropriators or by their agents"

5. "graduated sanctions" for rule violators

6. "conflict-resolution mechanisms [that] are readily available, low cost, and legitimate"

7. "minimal recognition of rights to organize"

8. "governance activities [being]...organized in multiple layers of nested enterprises." (Shackelford et Al, 2016)

3.2 Potential Governance and Policing Nodes

1. Internet users and user groups

Users can and do exert a very potent influence upon online behavior to enforce norms and report crime. Online forums and services expect and enforce acceptable behavior with the ability to limit access and ban individuals or larger groups of users. Individuals self-protect with spam, malware, and anti-virus protection, which in fact demonstrates the usefulness of nodal behavior as many of the AV and Spam protection software packages, report incidents first to the AV software vendor who then typically informs a wider audience via bulletins, blacklists, and reports to other interested groups.

2. Network Infrastructure Providers

Instructure Service Providers(ISP) act as another node through their written code of conduct or Terms of Service, which typically prohibit any criminal activity. Through the monitoring of their network, ISPs can and do detect many classes of cybercrime. Where the service provider is lax in enforcing conduct, we have seen nodal behavior from groups that provide information about an ISP and from the ISP's own customers who do not want to be blacklisted based on a ISP's lack of enforcement.

3. Corporate Entities

Non-ISP corporate entities enforce similar contractual obligations between both employees and vendors who provide services to those entities.

4. Non-governmental, non-police organizations

Many non-government organizations monitor internet activity and report to local, state, and federal agencies for potential action. These reporting agencies also disseminate information to the public. SANS ISC and SORBS are examples of non-governmental agencies that nevertheless investigate and report on cybercrime.

5. Government, non-police organizations

The Federal Trade Commission and other government agencies can fine and sanction businesses and individuals who use the internet to commit fraud or provide fraudulent information.

6. Police and Court

Whether at the local, state, or federal level, the formally recognized police are the only agencies that can apprehend and detain. The courts are the only mechanism that can determine guilt or innocence once charged.

4   SUMMARY AND CONCLUSION

While further research and refinement is required, we believe that the nodal form of governance within a polycentric framework is the basis attempting to address the difficulties of applying traditional policing methods to the cyberspace.

REFERENCES

[1] Broadhurst, R., Grabosky, P., Alazab, M., & Chon, S. (2014). Organizations and cybercrime: An analysis of the nature of groups engaged in cybercrime. International Journal of Cyber Criminology Vol 8 Issue 1 January - June 2014. Retrieved from http://www.cybercrimejournal.com/broadhurstetalijcc2014vol8issue1.pdf.

[2] Center for Strategic and International Studies. Retrieved from: https://www.mcafee.com/us/resources/reports/rp-economic-impact-cybercrime2.pdf.

[3] Dictionary.com (n.d.) 21st Century Lexicon. Retrieved June 7, 2017 from Dictionary.com website http://www.dictionary.com/browse/civil-society.

[4] Evans, D. (2012). Internet of Everything: It's the connections that matter. Retrieved from https://www.linkedin.com/pulse/20121201005511-122323-internet-of-everything-it-s-the-connections-that-matter.

[5] FBI's Internet Crime Complaint Center (IC3). (2014). 2014 Internet crime report. Retrieved from: https://pdf.ic3.gov/2014_IC3Report.pdf.

[6] Ghaus-Pasha, A. (2004). Role of civil society organizations in governance. Retrieved from: http://unpan1.un.org/intradoc/groups/public/documents/un/unpan019594.pdf.

[7] Goodman, M. (2015) Future crimes: Inside the digital underground and the battle for our connected world. Anchor Books, Penguin Random House Publishing LLC, New York, NY.

[8] Internet World Stats. (2016). Internet usage statistics for all the Americas. Mini-watts Marketing Group. Retrieved from: http://www.internetworldstats.com/stats2.htm.

[9] Kassem, L. (2016). 2016 Cybercrime reloaded: Our prediction for the year ahead. Security Intelligence – Analysis and insight for information security professionals. Retrieved from: https://securityintelligence.com/2016-cybercrime-reloaded-our-predictions-for-the-year-ahead/.

[10] Kohavi, L. (2015). Cybercrime in North America. Retrieved from: http://www.connect-world.com/index.php/magazines/north-america/item/26462-cybercrime-in-north-america.

[11] McAfee. (2014). Net losses: Estimating the global cost of cybercrime economic impact of cybercrime II.

[12] Murphy, J., and Roser, M. (2017). 'Internet'. Published online at OurWorld In Data.org. Retrieved from: https://ourworldindata.org/internet/.

[13] Paganini, P. (2012). Cybercrime evolution in North America and Western Europe. Retrieved from: http://securityaffairs.co/wordpress/8631/cyber-crime/cybercrime-evolution-in-north-america-and-western-europe.html.

[14] Pew Research Center. (2017). Internet/Broadband Fact Sheet. Retrieved from: http://www.pewinternet.org/fact-sheet/internet-broadband/.

[15] Ponemon Institute. (2014). Cost of cybercrime study: U.S. Hewlett-Packard. Retrieved from: https://ssl.www8.hp.com/us/en/ssl/leadgen/document_download.html?objid=4AA5-5208ENW (accessed October 24, 2014).

[16] Review, (2017). Forthcoming; Kelley School of Business Research Paper No. 16-6. Retrieved from SSRN: https://ssrn.com/abstract=2715799.

[17] Salamon, L. M., Anheier, H.K., List, R., Toepler, S., Sokolowski. S.W. (1999).

[18] Global Civil Society: Dimensions of the Nonprofit Sector, Johns Hopkins Center for Civil Society Studies Retrieved from: https://www.energizeinc.com/art/global-associational-revolution.

[19] Shackelford, Scott and Raymond, Anjanette and Balakrishnan, Rakshana and Dixit, Prakhar and Gjonaj, Julianna and Kavi, Rachith, When Toasters Attack: A Polycentric Approach to Enhancing the 'Security of Things' (January 14, 2016). University of Illinois Law.

[20] World Economic Forum (2013). World Scenario Series: The Future Role of Civil Society. Retrieved from: www.forum.org/docs/WEF_FutureRoleCivilSociety_Report_2013.pdf

Cybersecurity Career Profiling

Morgan Andreanna Zantua, M.A.
UW CIAC Director of Workforce Development

Barbara Endicott-Popovsky, Ph.D.
Ph.D. Executive Director UW CIAC

Abstract - Professionalization of a cybersecurity workforce is under development from multiple perspectives. Government agencies, the military and academic institutions strive to standardize excellent curriculum and career pathways, certifications, job descriptions classifications are contributing to the effort. In its infancy is the development of statistically validated psychological profiles of candidates' possessing the talent, disposition and interest to excel in the rapidly maturing field and diversifying field of cybersecurity. To address this gap, we propose to borrow from the well- established medical profession and utilize psychological profiling protocols tailoring a statistically validated career assessment tool to build cybersecurity psychological profiles of two markedly different cybersecurity career pathways. Once profiles are defined and validated we propose several Next Steps. Team members and industry partners comparing the psychological profiles can advise or refute a case to conduct additional profiling of additional cybersecurity career pathways. The assessment protocols and methodology will be disseminated to multiple communities at regional, national and international conferences to increase the diversity and numbers of talent entering the cybersecurity career pipeline.

1   INTRODUCTION

Talent demands discussed in the Human Capital Crisis in Cybersecurity in 2010 (Evans, 2010) are dwarfed by current projections for cybersecurity professionals. "The demand for these skilled workers is increasing enrollments in programs, but the demand will continue to grow as business computing increasingly moves toward the cloud." (Suciu, 2015). Jobs in cybersecurity grew

74% from 2007 to 2013 (Burning Glass Technologies, 2015) more than twice the growth rate of all IT jobs. While IT has been considered the entryway into cybersecurity, positions there are growing realization that the cybersecurity workforce shortage cannot rely on current IT programs or the existing IT workforce to meet the growing demand. As cybersecurity matures as an interdisciplinary profession, additional capabilities and knowledge beyond IT skills are required to perform and excel.

Initiatives to professionalize cybersecurity is underway. Research by Dr. Diana Burley, George Washington University Professor and Chair of Institute for Information Infrastructure Protection, compliments (Burley, 2014) extensive work by National Institute Education Training Programs (NIETP) to develop 2Y and 4Y+ educational program integrating Knowledge Units into curriculum while National Institute Cybersecurity Education (NICE) released for comment the NICE Cybersecurity Workforce Framework (NCWF) (Newhouse, 2016). Digitization's innovation impact private sector's workforce needs (Pental, 2017) with new security roles challenging the extensive task list presented in NCWF. The Department of Homeland Security's Cybersecurity Workforce Development Toolkit walks readers through a systemic approach to maturing their organization's cybersecurity workforce culture. (US Department of Homeland Security, 2016)

These major initiatives focus on the supply side of training and educating cybersecurity talent and the demand side of identifying career pathways, job descriptions and tasks performed by people working in cybersecurity jobs. However, to fully re-engineer the human capital crisis in cyber security, assessment tools are required to identify talent from multiple sources with the propensity to succeed in rapidly developing cyber security career pathways. The propensity to succeed describes candidates able to excel in learning acknowledged cybersecurity knowledge units and possess the psychological profile, temperament and interest, to thrive in the differentiated areas of cybersecurity. To meet the projected demands for a well-trained, competent cybersecurity workforce, identifying and nurturing cybersecurity talent nationally and providing career guidance to individuals within our country's borders is of the highest priority to meet the increasing need of high-quality cyber security professionals across multiple industries and economic sectors.

2 PREVIOUS WORK

Current challenges include identifying individuals with the combination of career training potential, and psychological profile to work in cyber security. Industry professionals acknowledge it takes more than 180 days to fill positions and 64% of applicants aren't qualified to perform required job functions. (ISACA, 2017) This industry survey mirrors conversations with leading academic researchers and a Chief Information Officer from a national laboratory; all commented on the need for more than people who just follow the check list. The demand is growing for critical thinkers who are adept at delivering cybersecurity to decision makers with diverse technical and non-technical backgrounds.

University of Maryland researchers and the Air Force are wrestling with similar issues. (Johnson, 2015) Initiatives to professionalize cybersecurity, meet the growing demand to fill the pipeline with more people, identify talent to guide individuals into the career pathway best suited to the psychological profile and contribute to the demand for this project.

The research team proposes to use a recent research study from the medical profession, a field professionalized 169 years ago to address this problem. Within the medical field, surgical specialties are highly competitive and lucrative professions. A research project to define a psychological profile for Surgical Burn Unit residents provides a lesson and protocol for selecting talent into cybersecurity.

In 2010 a team of psychologists published the "Psychological Profile of Surgeons and Surgical Residents (Foster, 2010) Twenty percent of surgical residents were not completing their residency at the Maricopa Burn Unit. This proved expensive to the surgical resident and exorbitant to the hospital. Hospital administration calculated the cost of $1,000,000 per failed resident. An Arizona State University research team developed a psychological profile overlaid on a performance curve developed from the pool of Attending Surgeons and Surgical Residents. Using approved Institutional Review Board standards, the World of Work Inventory (WOWI) was administered and the anonymized data utilized to build a psychological profile of high performing Attending Surgeons and Surgical Residents. The Surgical Psychological profile, built a profile to reflect the psychological profile of high performing surgeons suited to work in a Burn Unit. Since WOWI has been included and heeded during the selection process of Surgical Residents, the attrition rate dropped significantly, sparing residents from reapplying to different surgical programs, saving the hospital millions of dollars, increasing surgeon retention and improving patient satisfaction with medical treatment.

In recent decades medicine, as a mature profession, acknowledged psychological patterns connected to specializations (Reich, 1999) are defined. Cybersecurity proceeds towards professionalization and increasingly diverse career pathways are emerging. Intertwined with interdisciplinary implications requiring diverse skill sets and varied experiential backgrounds, the potential for varied psychological patterns and talent profiles are surfacing. (Pental, 2017)

KBP Pedagogical Model for IA Curriculum Development

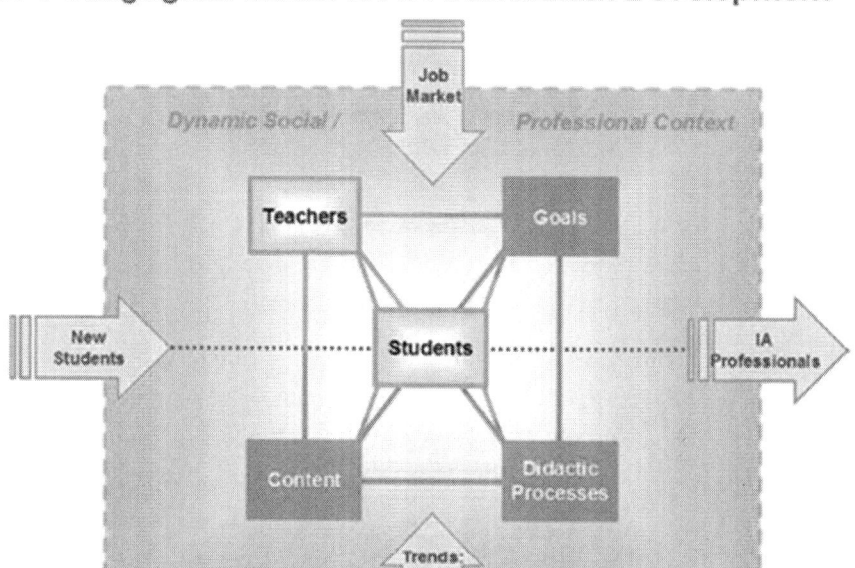

For the past fourteen years, researchers at the University of Washington using the KBP Pedagogical Model for IA Curriculum Development (Endicott-Popovsky, March 2014) have successfully transitioned 679 predominantly mid-career IT professionals into Information Assurance positions. The student centric KBG model accelerates the learning capabilities of students transitioning into cybersecurity and increases the supply of IA professionals by tapping into the stream of mid-career IT workers. In the early stages of research cycle outreach to non-IT professionals, transitioning military and non-traditional workers began. In 2010 researchers received multiple NSF grants. The Scholarship for Service grant supported the development of 17 cyber corps members to study cloud security and critical infrastructure. The second grant was based on VETS ENG GI Bill utilization to study transitioning Active Duty and National Guard service members to identify why more service members were not entering STEM (specifically cybersecurity) disciplines. (National Science Foundation, April 2009) During this study, university researchers interfaced with a team of workforce development professionals, transition specialists hired to provide career guidance and employment transition services to returning service members. Between 2009 to 2013, over 1,000 members of the military, Reserve, Guard and Active Duty received the same assessment tool used to profile surgical residents in the Maricopa Burn Unit study. For the purposes of the VETS ENG study, members received assessment, career coaching. During the year a cohort of 10 soldiers completed a graduate certificate in Information Assurance and Risk Management. Ninety percent of the study group obtained employment, additional certifications or degrees, including the cyber security related master degrees in Infrastructure Planning and Management, Information Management Systems and Cybersecurity and Leadership.

The university researchers collaborated with the workforce development transition coach incorporating additional career guidance, professional coaching coupled up with the student focused life-long learning methodology promoted as part of the Center for Academic Excellence's philosophy." Become a Professional" and 'finding your swim lane' within the cyber security career pathways allowing students to complete a WOWI and receive a coaching session based upon their customized profile. Feedback report in hand, students evaluate the career pathways and select areas of interest based in the NIST/NICE workforce framework matched to their career profile and interests. Their next step identifies gaps in their knowledge, certifications or education, as they personalize their cybersecurity tool kit. Students develop actionable strategies to close these gaps to make themselves competent, competitive and marketable for their targeted career specialty.

In response to the diversification of career pathways researcher and career coach proactively developed and included a specific career guidance and coaching module at the beginning of the first quarter in the three-quarter certificate. This module prepares all students, military, non-military, IT professionals and 'outliers' with a customized profile and an understanding of the emerging career pathways within cybersecurity. This clarity enables them to build a professional network from guest lecturers, speakers and industry experts participating in an Information Security risk management curriculum. Outliers refers to individuals entering the course without an IT degree. (ISLA Winner: Jennifer Chermoshnyuk, November 15, 2016) Based upon the student centric KBG model, adult learning theory and Bloom's Taxonomy, mid-career professionals mesh their industry specific knowledge with Information Assurance principles transitioning into positions of influence as cybersecurity concerns are being recognized across industry sectors. (Pental, 2017) Talented mid-career professionals from health care, law, logistics etc. recognizing the demand for a nationally recognized certificate in Information Assurance within their fields and gravitate to the program offered in–class and synchronously on-line.

The professionalization process of 'finding your swim lane' is also embedded into a current pilot in cooperative cybersecurity learning designed to close the gap between university/college graduation and acceptable professional performance on the job. Industry professionals acknowledge 'new' cybersecurity hires traditionally require 12 to 18 months' acclimation, workplace orientation and professional development before becoming strong contributors in the face paced cybersecurity workplace.

3   PROPOSED SOLUTION

The proposed solution to increasing the flow of individuals entering the ever increasing and diversifying cybersecurity professionals is the customization of a statistically validated multi-dimensional career assessment tool and career guidance protocol for broad distribution. Outreach to candidates from all stages of career development is aimed to identify those well suited to enter the cybersecurity field. A multilevel career focus can significantly address the number challenges corporate recruiters face due to widespread digitization.

Modeling elements within cybersecurity after the medical concepts is not uncommon. Implementing a systems theory approach, computer systems and human systems are subject to viruses and consist of multiple interrelated systems. From an antedoctal perspective, after administering over 350 assessments to individuals interested in cybersecurity, interesting trends in the Career Recommendation emerged. As expected a high percentage of candidates received recommendations at the bachelor degree level for Computer Network Architect, Data Base Manager and other IT related disciplines. Another segment of individuals received Epidemiology and Marriage Counselor as career recommendations.

Our research team proposes to implement a research study based upon the methodology engaged to develop psychological profiles of surgical residents well suited to working in the Maricopa burn unit. Current research preparations are underway to engage cybersecurity professionals working in corporate, government and military settings. One hundred and twenty individuals engaged in two distinctly different career pathways will be assessed with the career guidance instrument referenced earlier in the paper. Anonymized data tagged with organizational performance indicators will be normed to establish a post-dictive performance profile combining 34 variables arranged in three specific categories. In additional to five sub categories within career training potential, 12 categories within job satisfaction indicators combined with 17 career interest subscales.

4   CASE STUDIES

During the return of soldiers from Afghanistan and Iraq, an international collaboration with the British Columbia Institute of Technology (BCIT) addressed transitioning Canadian veterans into post-secondary programs. Utilizing several assessment tools, specifically the WOWI, and career guidance to interpret career recommendation reports with coaching sessions "led to the conclusion that a majority of the soldiers had both the ability and suitability to be successful as advanced placement students in business diploma programs.

(Wainwright, Spring 2015) Without this intervention these veterans intended to return to lower paying security work and laborer positions in their hometowns foregoing the opportunity of obtaining professional degrees.

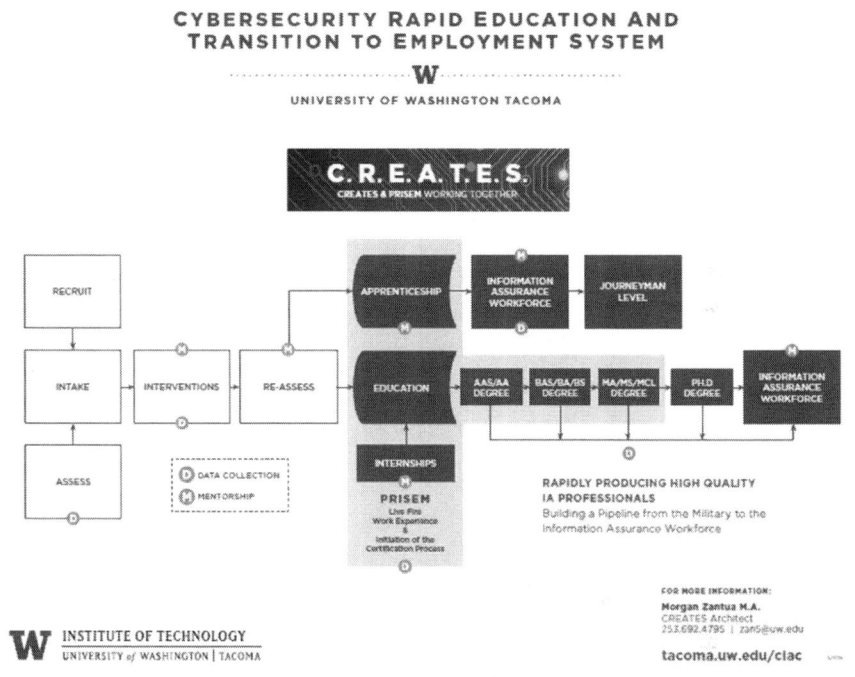

Over the course of three years the university research and workforce collaboration resulted in a model constructed to establish a pipeline of transitioning military personnel into cybersecurity careers. The model, Cybersecurity Rapid Employment Academic Training Employment System (CREATES), received funding to conduct outreach during the troop draw down of 2014-15. (Zantua, 2015) Funding supported outreach to 234 service members transitioning out of the military through the Soldier for Life program. Fifty percent (112) indicated an interest in cybersecurity careers, 176 completed the assessment tool and 100 veterans were tracked entering undergraduate and graduate level cybersecurity education programs. (Seifer, 2016). Current funding opportunities expand CREATES to target additional populations. RECREATES is the Reserve (US Army) Expansion of the CREATES model. Honing cybersecurity talent within the Reservists' ranks has strong workforce ramifications. Reservists are civilians the majority of their workdays, called to serve during time of the emergency and provide strength to Active Duty forces. Cybersecurity is identified internationally (Charlaff, 2014) and nationally as the new battleground. A current research project studies the impact of Cooperative Learning, CoCREATES, on ten university students engaged in work experience opportunities with a major telecommunications corporation.

5 EVALUATION

Two con-current research projects, CoCREATES and RECREATES, recently approved by the Institutional Review Board study16 US Army Reservists and 10 undergraduate/graduate students participating in a work experience as a pathway to employment with a major telecommunications corporation. The research focuses on methodologies to close the skills and knowledge gap and shorten preparation time of cybersecurity professionals. Built into the project design is a panel of nationally recognized experts comprised of representatives from two and four-year academic institutions, industry and military. The panel's guidance and insight will inform a flexible replicable model attractive for adaptation at other colleges and universities working to meet the increasing demand for cybersecurity professionals. A university based evaluator has been involved since the inception of the program.

6 DISCUSSION AND CONCLUSION

What are the implications of customizing an instrument to build statistically valid psychological and talent profiles of professionals successfully engaged in cybersecurity roles? Using these profiles would it be possible to identify potential cybersecurity talent from different sources and more diverse populations?

Defining and standardizing cybersecurity professionalization is a work in progress. This paper does not address industry certifications and work being done by professional organizations. Efforts are underway through the Center of Academic Excellence system to build in curricular standards and reach out to the K- 12 community[1] while a guide to current cybersecurity career pathways is out for comment to the community (Newhouse, 2016). Both initiatives are worthy efforts. Speaking with academic leaders in the field in the past decades' students have 'self-selected' themselves to enter cybersecurity. Whether it was the 12-year-old hacker or today, the student attracted to the 0% unemployment rate for cybersecurity professionals, (Pental, 2017), there are no definitive psychological talent profiles for this rapidly emerging profession. It is unchartered territory.

Through work conducted since 2009, having a multi-functional career/aptitude/psychological assessment tool coupled with a strong career guidance and coaching process is a gap in the system requiring attention. By multi-functional we refer to a tool capable of identifying aptitude, temperament and career interest to high school students deciding upon post-secondary career options, college students identifying a major related to their career future, adults transitioning between careers; and organizations seeking to attract new talent, identify and prepare incumbent workers for their cybersecurity workforce. Informed career decision making being when coached by a workforce development professional lays a foundation.

Defining profiles of two distinctly different career pathways is the first objective. Based upon the results of post-dictive assessments, the team and the

---

[1] https://www.nsa.gov/resources/students/summer-camps/gencyber/

evaluator will be in a position to compare and contrast the similarities and differences between the two career pathways. Conversations with corporate partners to identify high demand and dissimilar pathways are underway. Further profiling of additional cybersecurity career pathways would be contingent upon the differences discovered through the initial psychological profiles and future funding. A cybersecurity focus coaching protocol is the second objective. Guidance counselors, coaches and human resource professionals trained in delivery of cybersecurity career development protocols will benefit the organization and the individual. Understandably, not everyone will have a cybersecurity career oriented profile but trained professionals armed with insights from a targeted tool can identify and nurture people with a propensity for cybersecurity career pathways. In the course of this nurturing, the mere mention of the diversity of careers in cybersecurity could help close the gap in the supply and demand of people entering the field. Cybersecurity career development is currently behind the curve in this rapidly emerging field. The initial work proposed, research based assessment tools and coaching protocols, can lay a foundation for outreach across populations to identify undiscovered talent.

7 FUTURE WORK

Dissemination of results defining the outcomes of the cybersecurity career profiling initiative comes next. Presenting results and protocols at targeted conferences to share the cybersecurity psychological profiles research includes an invitational challenge to corporations, high schools, colleges, universities and transitional worker programs to implement the assessment/coaching protocol. Included in the invitation is the suggestion to consider collaborative long-term cybersecurity career studies measuring the impact of identifying cybersecurity career profiles in candidates provided by the assessment and career guidance counseling. Application of initial cybersecurity/psychological profiles will be incorporated into program recruitment protocols. Further validation of profiles will inform future profiling initiatives to other cybersecurity career pathways.

REFERENCES

[1]   Burley, D. E. (2014). Would cybersecurity professionalization help address the cybeersecurity crisis? ACM, 24-27.

[2]   Burning Glass Technologies. (2015). *Job Market Intelligence: Cybersecurity Jobs, 2015.* http://burning-glass.com/wp-content/uploads/Cybersecurity_Jobs_Report_2015.pdf.

[3]   Charlaff, J. (2014). Cyberspace: The New Battleground. A Perspective from Israel. *Homeland Security Today.us*, pp. http://www.hstoday.us/columns/critical-issues-in-national-cybersecurity/blog/cyberspace-the-new-battleground-a-perspective-from-israel/1a663de30bef13199d8bf8be34f9a648.html.

[4]   Endicott-Popovsky, B. P. (March 2014). Application of pedagogical fundamentals for the holistic development of cybersecurity professionals. *ACM Inroads*, 57-68.

[5]   Evans, K. R. (2010). *A Human Capital Crisis in Cybersecurity: Technical Proficiency Matters.* Center for Strategic Initiatives.

[6]   Foster, K. N.-R. (2010). A Psychological Profile of Surgeons and Surgical Residents. *APDS Spring Meeting.*

[7]   ISACA. (2017). *State of Cybersecurity 2017: Current Trends in Workforce Development.* https://www.isaca.org/cyber/Documents/state-of-cybersecurity-2017_res_eng_0217.pdf: ISACA.

[8]   ISLA Winner: Jennifer Chermoshnyuk. (November 15, 2016). http://www.itsecuritynews.info/isla-winner-jennifer-chermoshnyuk/.

[9]   Johnson, N. (2015). The Air Force has a plan for testing cyber aptitutde. *Gov Loop*, https://www.govloop.com/the-air-force-has-a-plan-for-testing-cyber-aptitude/.

[10] National Science Foundation. (April 2009). *Veterans' Education for Engineering and Science: Report of the National Science Foundation Workshop on Enhancing the Post 9/11 Veterans Educational Benefit.* http://www.nsf.gov/eng/eec/VeteranEducation.pdf.

[11] Newhouse, B. K. (2016). *NICE Cybersecurity Workforce Framework (NCWF).* NIST, US Department of Commerce.

[12] Pental, S. (2017). 10 New Information Security Roles for the Digitization Era. 24-26.

[13] Reich, D. U. (1999). The relationship of cognitivie, personality, and academic measures to anesthesiology resident clinical performance. *Anesth Analg.*, 1092-1100.

[14] Seifer, A. (2016). *Matopma; Omstotite pf Standards and Technology Technical Progress Report.* NIST Award No 60NANB14D229.

[15] Suciu, P. (2015, Sept 9). Cybersecurity's ever-growing brain drain. *Fortune Tech*, pp. http://fortune.com/2015/09/09/cyber-securitys-ever-growing-brain-drain/.

[16] US Department of Homeland Security. (2016). *Cybersecurity Workforce Development Toolkit: How to Build a Strong Cybersecurity Workforce.*

[17] Wainwright, K. F. (Spring 2015). An Alternative Approach to Prior Learning and Advanced Placement in Post Secondary Programs for Veterans. The Canadian Experience. *The Colloquium for Information System Security Education Special Edition: Educational Approaches to Transition former Military Personnel into the Cybersecurity Field*, 12-34.

[18] Zantua, M. D.-P. (2015). Re-Engineering the Cybersecurity Human Capital Crisis: *Educational Approaches to Transition Former Military Personnel into the Cybersecurity Field Special Edition of the Colloquium for Information System Security Education (CISSE)*, 156-152.

Journal of The Colloquium for Information System Security Education (CISSE)
Edition 5, Issue 1 – October 2017

Erich Spengler
Student Paper of the Year for 2017

Cybersecurity Training and the End-User: Pathways to Compliance

Dinesh Reddy
dinesh.reddy@utsa.edu

Glenn Dietrich
glenn.dietrich@utsa.edu

The University of Texas at San Antonio
1, UTSA Circle, San Antonio TX 78249

Abstract - In order to effectively combat cybersercurity threats at home and in organizations, it is imperative to achieve higher end-user cybersecurity compliance. Cybersecurity training is generally accepted as a means to increase compliance behavior. Training can influence compliance by one or more of three causal pathways: by increasing cybersecurity awareness, by increasing cybersecurity proficiency (i.e., improve cybersecurity skills) and by raising cybersecurity self-efficacy. The effects of awareness and self-efficacy on compliance have been empirically examined and reported in literature, but the effect of cybersecurity skills has not received much attention. In an effort to understand the pathways through which training affects compliance, we develop a theoretical model and offer propositions. The model helps us understand how cybersecurity training should be designed and executed to optimally influence each of the three pathways to compliance and finally to have an optimal impact on compliance. Empirical validation will be performed at a later stage. Results of the study are expected to help design training programs to enhance end-user cybersecurity skills and consequently cybersecurity compliance.

Categories and Subject Descriptors

K.5.2 [Legal Aspects of Computing]: *Governmental Issues – Regulation*

General Terms

Training, Security

Keywords

Cybersecurity training, cybersecurity skill, cybersecurity awareness, self-efficacy in information security, cybersecurity compliance

1 INTRODUCTION

"...the human remains the weakest link in the information security chain." (Eric Savitz, 2011)

The idea that the end-user is the weakest link in the security chain has been repeated by many scholars and practitioners. There are some who object to this perspective arguing that it is used as a cover for the failure to design effective and usable safeguards. Regardless of whether one believes that users are the weakest link, it must be accepted that end-user behavior can often lead to lapses in security. Such lapses are often attributed to a lack of awareness of security issues. For instance, a SANS institute report suggests that "A Security Awareness program is probably the most important weapon in the Information Security professional's arsenal." (SANS Institute, 2001). Awareness programs provide guidelines such as use strong passwords, use a different password for each account, do not post the password on the computer screen and so on, but fail to educate the user on other issues, such as interpreting warning messages and responding appropriately. Savitz (2011) remarks, "We're all familiar with the obscure "certificate warnings" that our Web browsers occasionally grace us with – these warnings are completely indecipherable, un-actionable, and thus routinely ignored." This suggests that cybersecurity training programs may need to go beyond simple awareness education. Our research is based on the premise that training needs to include sufficient knowledge to understand messages and know what responses are appropriate, and, the development of skills to execute the steps to protect the information residing in the computer in the event of a threat.

End-user training is recognized as an important component of the steps necessary to improve cybersecurity compliance, and consequently cybersecurity posture. Antecedents of cybersecurity compliance in both the home and organizational context have been studied. Among the individual factors that have been examined are cybersecurity awareness, self-efficacy in information security and, to a lesser extent, cybersecurity skills. Each of these variables is potentially a mediator between cybersecurity training and compliance. Research has not examined either the mediating role of these three factors, nor has it examined the relative effectiveness of these measures in achieving compliance. Hence the research questions that will be pursued in our research are:

1. What factors mediate the relationship between cybersecurity training and compliance?

2. What is the relative effectiveness of each factor on improving compliance?

3. How does the nature of training affect each of the mediating variables?

In the current article, we develop the research model and provide supporting arguments for the relationships proposed.

The rest of the article is organized in the following manner: First, we present literature review on key concepts related to cybersecurity compliance, training, awareness, self-efficacy in information security and cybersecurity skills followed by the propositions and the research model. Next, we discuss the proposed methodology to test the research model. Finally, we conclude with practical implications and future research.

2 LITERATURE REVIEW

2.1 Cybersecurity Compliance (CC)

End user CC is a specific case of cybersecurity behavior in which computer users show conformity with the safe and secure rules and policies, and comply with a recommended course of action (Johnston and Warkentin 2010, Herath and Rao 2009). Table-1 provides a summary of a sample of studies in which CC is the dependent variable. There are several points that can be seen in the table. First, cybersecurity compliance has been studied both in organizational and home context. In organizational context, the studies have been conducted at both organizational and individual level of analysis. In the home context, studies have been at the individual level of analysis. The model that is being developed in our research is for the individual level of analysis, and should be applicable in both the home and organizational context.

CC is difficult to achieve for many reasons. For example, Herath and Rao (2009) state that computer users are most likely to discard the secure rules and policies as mere steps and guidelines, rather than considering the secure policies as standards that help achieve cybersecurity. CC is critical since the negligence and non-compliance by individuals and employees of an organization will lead to significant financial losses caused by data breaches (PrivacyRights website 2016).

Several predictors of CC have been studied in prior research, such as fear deterrence, fear appeals, user awareness and so on. The effectiveness of the antecedents is likely to vary based on the motivation of the users to comply or conform to security policies. Users can be classified into unwilling conformers, reluctant conformers and the willing conformers. Unwilling conformers need effective deterrence measures to motivate them. The reluctant conformers may be motivated by fear appeals, social influence, threat perception and so on. Willing conformers are motivated to comply with cybersecurity guidelines and policies, but may be hampered by their lack of awareness of potential threats, their lack of understanding of security related issues, and their lack of skills to take the necessary steps to protect information assets. In the current study, our focus is on enabling the willing conformers to achieve a stronger security posture through appropriate training. In Table 1, it can be seen that awareness has received much attention, self-efficacy has received some attention and cybersecurity skills have only recently received some attention, suggesting the need for more research on these factors.

Compliance as DV Papers	Level	Context	Predictors of Compliance
Rhee et al. 2009	Individual	Home	Self-efficacy in information security, computer/internet experience, security breach incidents, general controllability.
Johnston & Warkentin 2010.	Individual	Org	Fear appeals, self-efficacy, response efficacy, threat severity, social influence.
Bulgurcu et al. 2010	Individual	Org	Information security awareness.
D'Arcy et al. 2009	Org	Org	User Awareness of security countermeasures, sanction perceptions.

Compliance as DV Papers	Level	Context	Predictors of Compliance
Herath & Rao 2009	Individual	Org	Severity of penalty, certainty of detection, Normative beliefs, peer behavior, perceived effectiveness.
Lee et al. 2004	Org	Org	General deterrence factors such as security policies and security awareness.
Blanke 2008	Individual	Org	Computer security policy awareness.

Table-1 Summary of Past Literature on Cybersecurity Compliance

2.2 Cybersecurity Training (CT)

In business environments, the need for the implementation of security countermeasures such as CT has been emphasized and recommended in order to reduce IS computer abuse (Straub and Welke 1998). Security policies form the basis for security education training and awareness (SETA). CT sessions in general are aimed at informing the users about unacceptable system use and penalties for noncompliance (Straub 1990). CT is defined as those activities that impart specific cyber skills such as safe internet browsing, encryption, decryption and system manipulation (Torkzadeh and Van Dyke 2002), in order to make security decisions (Furman et al. 2011). The ultimate goal of CT is to impart knowledge and skills such as vulnerability analysis and mitigation, intrusion detection and incident response, in order to be less susceptible to social engineering.

Some of the common training techniques include formal training, passive computer-based and web-based training, and interactive computer-based training (Cone et al. 2007). The different aspects of training effectiveness are evaluated using measures such as reaction, learning, cognitive, and behavioral criteria. (Frayne and Latham 1987). The reaction criteria measure the extent to which trainees liked the training content, and the perceived relevance of the training to trainee's needs. The learning criteria assess the knowledge and skills gained during the training. Prior computer knowledge, computer experience, computer playfulness, and performance during training are all shown to affect post-training effectiveness (Potosky 2002, Puhakeinen and Siponen 2010). However, two studies were identified that examined the effect of CT on CC and the results of these studies are mixed as shown in Table 2.

Study	Training Increase Compliance	Key Finding	Metho dology	Sample
Lee et al. 2004	No	Self-defense intention (SDI) arising out of training increases computer abuse.	Survey	500 MBA students and 500 middle managers in six companies in Korea.
Straub 1990	Yes	Training sessions reduce abuse.	Survey	IS directors. Middle IS managers, IS security officers, controllers, auditors,

Study	Training Increase Compliance	Key Finding	Metho dology	Sample
				programmers, analysts, etc.

Table-2 Summary of Past Literature on Cybersecurity Training

2.3 Cybersecurity Awareness (CA)

CA is defined as the state of being cognizant of performing secure tasks on a computer (Bulgurcu et al. 2010). Studies have focused on different aspects of awareness. For instance, some have examined awareness of computer usage policies (e.g., Cronan et al. 2006), others have examined security countermeasures (e.g., D'Arcy et al. 2009) and so on. The multiple aspects collectively include comprehensive information about general guidelines of information security, basic education on security risks and consequences of cybersecurity threats, and tracking internet usage for abnormal activities (Choi et al. 2013). All awareness aspects listed in table-3 can be categorized into three dimensions. One such dimension of awareness is related to security policies where a computer user is aware that there are detailed set of guidelines to guide the user in understanding what actions on computers are safe and secure (D'Arcy et al. 2009). Another dimension of awareness refers to trainings where a computer user is aware that there are training programs available to educate users on acceptable safe and secure usage of computers, and the risks involved in misusing the computers. Yet another dimension of awareness refers to tracking internet usage by service providers where a computer user is aware that their computer activities are under surveillance and that any misuse of computer will be detected as unusual behavior (Choi et al. 2013). Table-3 lists past studies on the effect of CA on CC, and the results are mixed at best.

Compliance as DV Papers	Cybersecurity Awareness Aspect	Awareness Increases Compliance?
Bulgurcu et al. 2010	Information security awareness	Yes
D'Arcy et al. 2009	User awareness of security countermeasures	No
Aytes and Connolly 2004	Awareness of safe practice, awareness of negative consequences	No
Dinev and Hu 2007	Technology Awareness	Yes
Lee et al. 2004	Security awareness	No
Cronan et al. 2006	Awareness of computer usage policies	No
Foltz et al. 2005	Awareness of computer usage policies	No
Choi et al. 2013	Cybersecurity countermeasures awareness	No

Table-3 Summary of Past Literature on Cybersecurity Awareness

2.4 Self-Efficacy in Information Security (SEIS)

The perception of efficacy as per Witte (1994) includes the cognitions of the efficacy of recommended response and the efficacy of the individual in performing that response. The latter is known as self-efficacy and is defined as the degree to which individuals believe in their abilities to organize and execute a particular course of action (Bandura 1986; Vishwanath et al. 2011), and enact the recommended response (Johnston and Warkentin 2010). Self-efficacy is people's belief in their abilities to mobilize the motivation, cognitive resources, and courses of action needed to exercise control over given events and perform the tasks successfully (Ozer and Bandura, 1990). Ng et al. (2009) defines self-efficacy in terms of an individual's self-confidence in his/her ability to perform a behavior. Social cognitive theory has self-efficacy as an important construct, which is a form of self-evaluation that is nearest determinant of individual behavior, and also influences the amount of initiation, effort, self-regulation and persistence of coping efforts to overcome obstacles (Bandura 1986). Bandura (1977) identified four important factors that affect self-efficacy beliefs as listed in table-4.

Factor	Description
Enactive experience	Self-efficacy is increased by performing a behavior successfully.
Vicarious experience	Self-efficacy is increased when other people holding similar interests of that of an individual are performing a behavior successfully.
Verbal persuasion	Self-efficacy is influenced by encouragement and discouragement pertaining to an individual's performance.

Factor	Description
psychological and affective states	Self-efficacy is influenced by an individual's own anxiety and stress

Table-4 Self-Efficacy Model (Bandura 1977)

Computer self-efficacy (CSE) which is derived from self-efficacy is defined as an individual's judgment of his/her capability to use a computer in various situations (Compeau and Higgins 1995; Vishwanath et al. 2011). Marakas et al. (1998) explains the concept of CSE at 'general level' that applies to multiple computer domains and 'task specific level' which applies to specific computer-related tasks within the domain of general computing. Adapting the general definition of CSE to the more specific information security context, SEIS is defined as a belief in an individual's capability to protect information systems from unauthorized disclosure, loss, modification, destruction and lack of availability (Rhee et al. 2009). SEIS refers to an individual's self-confidence in his/her abilities in practicing computer security that is likely to increase computer security behavior (Ng et al. 2009). SEIS is also defined as the user's confidence in taking the safeguarding measure and is an important determinant of threat avoidance motivation (Liang and Xue 2009; Liang and Xue 2010).

SEIS is examined as a direct determinant of behavioral intent of end user CC (Johnston and Warkentin 2010). Self-efficacy is one of the most popular variables found by the systematic review of research on variables that affect compliance with information security policies of organizations (Sommestad et al. 2014). It was also found that while each of the 40 variables was only investigated in a single study, self-efficacy was investigated in 7 studies. Two studies also proved consistent results in linking self-efficacy with actual compliance (Sommestad et al. 2014). Prior studies have examined very few antecedents to SEIS. Johnston and Warkentin (2010) have shown the impact of perceptions of threat severity to be negative on SEIS. Results from the same study also show the impact of threat susceptibility to be positive on SEIS. Rhee et al. (2009) have examined the effect of prior experience in computers and internet, security breach incidents and general controllability of information security threats on SEIS.

2.5 Cybersecurity Skills (CS)

Skill is defined as "a combination of ability, knowledge and experience that enables a person to do something well" (Boyatzis and Colb 1991: pg280). On similar lines, Torkzadeh and Lee (2003) define skill as the ability to understand and apply the intellectual abilities to accomplish the most appropriate action for the best result. Skills influence an individual's experience, behavior and attitude (Choi et al. 2013) and increase efficiency and positive behavior (Carruth et al. 2010). End user computing skill is referred to as an ability to utilize computer software and hardware in order to design, develop, modify and maintain applications for task-related activities. One specific form of computing skill is defined by Torkzadeh and Lee (2003) as IT skill, which is the knowledge and ability to use computer software, hardware and procedures for specific computer application development. On similar lines, we derive yet another specific form of computing skill to be CS, which encompass the capability to effectively utilize computer security programs such as antivirus programs. Hence, computing skills form the foundation of CS, since an appropriate level of computing skills is needed to effectively learn and utilize the cybersecurity knowledge.

Extending the definition of end user computing skill given by Torkzadeh and Lee (2003) to cybersecurity domain, CS is defined as the capability to practically apply intellectual abilities such as cybersecurity tools (e.g., anti-virus, anti-spyware) in order to protect the sensitive data stored in a computer (Rezgui and Marks 2008). CS can represent either technical abilities or non-technical abilities or a combination of both. Technical abilities involve utilizing technical knowledge and experience on software and hardware needed for performing secure activities on computers (Lerouge et al. 2005) and to effectively utilize cybersecurity innovations and functions. Applying this concept, Lerouge et al. (2005) studied the appropriateness of skill set of a systems analyst in order to effectively utilize and explore technology. They found the relevance between each skill dimensions and the role played in utilizing that skill. Non-technical abilities involve motivational factors from within a user to seek out the most appropriate knowledge that is needed to safeguard the computer, and repeatedly performs the secure actions in order to gain cybersecurity experience without being aware of the technical details (Rank et al. 2004, Dworkin et al. 2003). In the current article, we limit the term CS to the technical skills only.

3   RESEARCH MODEL[1] AND PROPOSITIONS

Training has been generally shown to have an improvement in the awareness levels. Training is the universal panacea recommended to raise security awareness (e.g., Brodie 2008). Furthermore, there is empirical evidence to support that training improves awareness levels (Eminagaoglu et al. 2009). Hence,

> *Proposition 1a: Cybersecurity training positively influences cybersecurity awareness.*

The need for CA to increase CC has been argued in both the academic venue (Siponen 2000) and the commercial venue (NICCS 2015). But empirical evidence of the effect of CA on CC has been mixed as discussed earlier in table-3. The causal link between CA and CC in our model is being argued on a

---

[1] The proposed model subsumes an earlier model (relating CA, CC and CS) that we have published at another venue.

logical basis rather than on the basis of empirical evidence. Users who are unaware of the existence of cybersecurity problems are unlikely to seek solutions for them. Further, users who lack an awareness of solutions will fail to take necessary steps to ensure cybersecurity.

Proposition 1b: Cybersecurity awareness will positively influence cybersecurity compliance.

Computer training has been shown to affect CSE by determining multiple levels of CSE (Cassidy and Eachus 2002). Studies have also shown that training has a positive effect on self-efficacy and that post training, self-efficacy positively affects performance (Gist et al. 1989, Torkzadeh et al. 1999, Marakas et al. 1998). On the basis of this, it can be argued that CT will influence SEIS.

Proposition 2a: Cybersecurity training will positively influence self-efficacy in information security.

Individuals with higher SEIS also have stronger intentions to strengthen cybersecurity. Johnston and Warkentin (2010) have shown that SEIS has a positive effect on an individual's intentions to adopt recommended computer security actions. Rhee et al. (2009) have shown that individuals with higher SEIS tend to use more security protection software and demonstrate more security conscious behavior. Individuals with higher SEIS also have stronger intentions to put more effort to strengthen cybersecurity (Rhee et al. 2009).

Proposition 2b: Self-efficacy in information security will positively influence cybersecurity compliance.

Computer training experiences have been shown to enhance the skill set of a computer user both at individual and organizational level (Marakas et al. 1998).

Proposition 3a: Cybersecurity training will positively influence cybersecurity skills.

The skills theory posits that in any field, a specific skill results in specific cognitive development that directly affects behavior. If the cognitive development happens in a sequence, then a particular skill is controlled on each developmental sequence, and each skill gradually goes up from one level to another in the developmental sequence (Fischer 1980). This implies that as the developmental levels go higher the resulting skill structure, will have an incremental effect on the behavior. The behavior is not uniform across all developmental levels due to difference in the skill structure. Udo et al., (2010) apply this concept to learning process in web services field, where the learning process captures unique inclinations of customers and individual differences in skill levels. Carlton and Levy (2015) take a similar approach and state that a skill is acquired over a period of time in three stages from initial acquisition of knowledge to converting that into procedural knowledge which is more organized, and progressing towards an experienced level. Extending this to the area of cybersecurity, it can be argued that CT will increase CS. In the case of motivated conforming users, if users possess high levels of the necessary CS to comply, then CC will be correspondingly high. If users do not possess adequate skills, then compliance will be correspondingly low. On the basis of this, it can be stated that CC will be positively correlated to CS. Combining the relationships between CS and CC, it can be said that:

Proposition 3b: Cybersecurity skills will positively influence cybersecurity compliance.

Studies show that awareness in general improves self-efficacy. For instance, awareness has been shown to significantly increase internet and computer self-efficacy (Torkzadeh et al. 2006). Rezgui and Marks (2008) mention that regular update on security policies and relevant awareness initiatives will prevent users from underestimating the dangers caused by their actions. Such cognizance will enhance the confidence of users in relation to security-related matters. This leads us to the next proposition.

Proposition 4: Cybersecurity awareness will positively influence self-efficacy in information security.

The ability to learn a computer skill and being proficient in using that skill is closely related to computer self-efficacy (Compeau and Higgins 1995; McCoy 2010). Skills closely relate to self-efficacy and individual reactions to technology usage and adoption (Compeau et al. 1999). Studies also found that both computer proficiency and computer self-efficacy are results of user's skill level development and transformation (Fischer 1980; McCoy 2010). Choi et al. (2013) has shown that an individual's ability to detect and remove suspicious malware software hidden in the computer is significantly correlated to the same individual's perceptions about his/her ability to detect and remove suspicious malware software hidden in the computer. This leads us to the following propositions that relate CS and SEIS.

Proposition 5: Cybersecurity skills positively influence self-efficacy in information security.

The effect of CA on CC may be mixed. In particular, a user who is aware of a solution but is not proficient to implement the solution may fail to comply with the necessary cybersecurity steps. In contrast, a user who is aware of the solution and has the necessary skills to implement the solution will succeed in complying. Thus, it can be seen that CS has a moderating effect on the relationship between CA and CC.

Proposition 6a: Cybersecurity skills will moderate the effect of cybersecurity awareness on cybersecurity compliance.

Similarly, a user who has high self-efficacy but low level of skills may not be able to comply with security requirements. In contrast, a user who has high self-efficacy and high level of skills will be able to comply. In effect, security will moderate the effect of SEIS on CC.

Proposition 6b: Cybersecurity will moderate the effect of self-efficacy in information security on compliance

Figure-1 shows the research model based on the propositions which will be tested empirically.

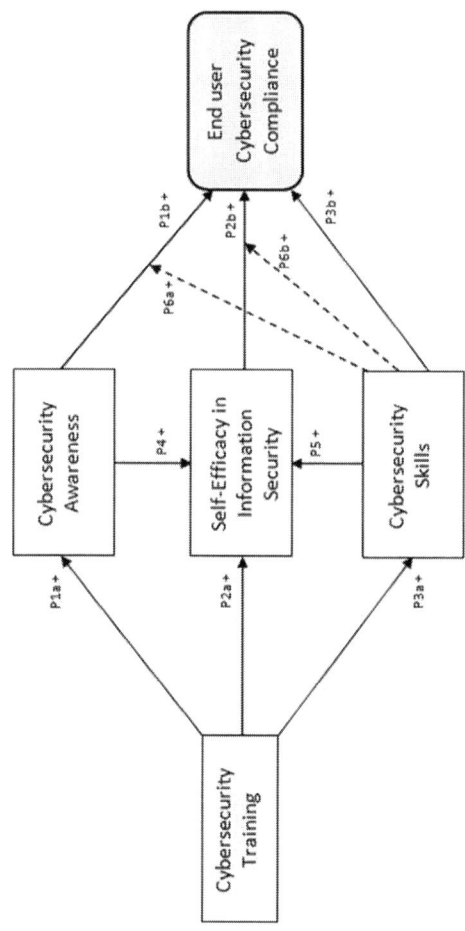

Figure-1 Research model

4 PROPOSITION METHODOLOGY

Survey methodology is planned to empirically validate our proposed research model. Survey items will be adopted from past research and suitable modifications will be made as applicable to this study. Initial survey items will be reviewed by experts in the field. Reliabilities and content validities of all survey items will be ensured before the items are used in actual data collection. Target population for this study will be university undergraduate and graduate students, and other computer users in a large academic setting.

Structural equation modeling using partial least squares (PLS-SEM) path coefficients will be used to conduct empirical data analysis to test for main effects, mediation and interaction effects of moderators. Factor analysis will be used to determine the item loadings on the respective constructs thus ensuring content validity of the survey items. Internal consistency tests will also be checked by using cronbach's alpha reliability. VIF test will be performed to ensure that multicollinearity is not an issue. Table-5 shows sample survey items for each construct.

5 CONCLUSION

The purpose of this article is to develop a research model and draw propositions to better understand the pathways through which CT affects CC. Using past literature, we present a model where CA, SEIS and CS are conceptualized as mediators between CT and CC. We also draw key relationships among CA, CS and SEIS in order to increase the explanatory power of the model. Also, CS is modeled as a moderator of the relationship between CA and CC, and between SEIS and CC. The propositions will be tested empirically by administering a survey instrument on computer end users. The use of self-report measurements is a limitation, but such models are difficult to test using other research methods such as experiments. Also, some measures such as compliance are difficult to observe directly.

It is anticipated that the results will demonstrate the importance of the need for technical skills in end-users to improve CC. Literature has emphasized the role of awareness and self-efficacy but has not paid sufficient attention to CS. We believe that while awareness and self-efficacy are important, but their effects will be weak in the absence of technical skills. Our program of research is aimed at testing this belief empirically, and encouraging greater attention to the development of CS among end-users. Our intention is to begin by creating theory-based cybersecurity training materials. These materials will be used to validate the model presented here, and subsequently used to help develop security skills in end-users.

Construct	Sample Survey Item	Response Range
CC	I use anti-spyware software currently. (adapted from Johnston and Warkentin 2010)	Strongly disagree to Strongly Agree
CT	I have received some form of training to protect my computer from attacks. (Self-developed)	Strongly disagree to Strongly Agree
CA	I am aware of the spyware problems and consequences. (Dinev and Hu 2007)	Strongly disagree to Strongly Agree
SEIS	I feel confident handling virus infected files. (Rhee et al. 2009)	No skill to leading performer

Construct	Sample Survey Item	Response Range
CS	I have the skills to detect and remove computer virus and worm (adapted from Choi et al. 2013)	No skill to leading performer

Table-5 Sample Survey Items

REFERENCES

[1] Aytes, K., & Connolly, T. (2005). Computer security and risky computing practices: A rational choice perspective. *Advanced topics in end user computing, 4,* 257.

[2] Bandura, A. (1986). *Social foundations of thought and action* (pp. 5-107). Prentice Hall.: Englewood Cliffs, NJ.

[3] Bandura, A. (1977). Self-efficacy: toward a unifying theory of behavioral change. *Psychological review, 84*(2), 191.

[4] Blanke, S. J. (2008). *A Study of the Contributions of Attitude, Computer Security Policy Awareness, and Computer Self-Efficacy to the Employees' Computer Abuse Intention in Business Environments* (Doctoral dissertation, Nova Southeastern University).

[5] Boyatzis, R. E., & Kolb, D. A. (1991). Assessing individuality in learning: The learning skills profile. *Educational Psychology, 11*(3-4), 279-295.

[6] Brodie, C. (2008). The importance of security awareness training, https://www.sans.org/reading-room/whitepapers/awareness/importance-security-awareness-training-33013 (last visited: Apr 14, 2017)

[7] Bulgurcu, B., Cavusoglu, H., & Benbasat, I. (2010). Information security policy compliance: an empirical study of rationality-based beliefs and information security awareness. *MIS Quarterly, 34*(3), 523-548.

[8] Carlton, M., & Levy, Y. (2015). Expert assessment of the top platform independent cybersecurity skills for non-IT professionals. In *SoutheastCon 2015* (pp. 1-6). IEEE.

[9] Carruth, A. K., Pryor, S., Cormier, C., Bateman, A., Matzke, B., & Gilmore, K. (2010). Evaluation of a School - Based Train - the - Trainer Intervention Program to Teach First Aid and Risk Reduction Among High School Students. *Journal of school health, 80*(9), 453-460.

[10] Cassidy, S., & Eachus, P. (2002). Developing the computer user self-efficacy (CUSE) scale: Investigating the relationship between computer self-efficacy, gender and experience with computers. *Journal of Educational Computing Research, 26*(2), 133-153.

[11] Choi, M., Levy, Y., & Hovav, A. (2013). The Role of User Computer Self-Efficacy, Cybersecurity Countermeasures Awareness, and Cybersecurity Skills

Influence on Computer Misuse. In *Proc. of the Pre-Int. Conference of Inform. Syst.(ICIS) SIGSEC–Workshop on Inform. Security and Privacy (WISP) 2013*.

[12] Compeau, D. R., & Higgins, C. A. (1995). Computer self-efficacy: Development of a measure and initial test. *MIS Quarterly*, 189-211.

[13] Compeau, D., Higgins, C. A., & Huff, S. (1999). Social cognitive theory and individual reactions to computing technology: A longitudinal study. *MIS Quarterly*, 145-158.

[14] Cone, B. D., Irvine, C. E., Thompson, M. F., & Nguyen, T. D. (2007). A video game for cyber security training and awareness. *computers & security, 26*(1), 63-72.

[15] Cronan, T. P., Foltz, C. B., & Jones, T. W. (2006). Piracy, computer crime, and IS misuse at the university. *Communications of the ACM, 49*(6), 84-90.

[16] D'Arcy, J., Hovav, A., & Galletta, D. (2009). User awareness of security countermeasures and its impact on information systems misuse: a deterrence approach. *Information Systems Research, 20*(1), 79-98.

[17] Dinev, T., & Hu, Q. (2007). The centrality of awareness in the formation of user behavioral intention toward PIT. *Journal of the Association for Information Systems, 8*(7), 23.

[18] Dworkin, J. B., Larson, R., & Hansen, D. (2003). Adolescents' accounts of growth experiences in youth activities. *Journal of youth and adolescence*, 32(1), 17-26.

[19] Eminagaoglu, M., Ucar, E., and Eren, S. (2009). The positive outcomes of information security awareness training in companies – *A case study, Information Security Technical Report*, 14, 223-229.

[20] Eric Savitz. (2011) (http://www.forbes.com/sites/ciocentral/2011/11/03/humans-the-weakest-link-in-information-security/#7e48cb2d31fd, last visited May 4, 2016)

[21] Fischer, K. W. (1980). A theory of cognitive development: The control and construction of hierarchies of skills. *Psychological review, 87*(6), 477.

[22] Foltz, C. B., Paul Cronan, T., & Jones, T. W. (2005). Have you met your organization's computer usage policy?. *Industrial Management & Data Systems, 105*(2), 137-146.

[23] Frayne, C. A., & Latham, G. P. (1987). Application of social learning theory to employee self-management of attendance. *Journal of applied psychology, 72*(3), 387.

[24] Furman, S. M., Theofanos, M. F., Choong, Y. Y., & Stanton, B. (2011). Basing cybersecurity training on user perceptions. *IEEE Security & Privacy*, (2), 40-49.

[25] Gist, M. E., Schwoerer, C., & Rosen, B. (1989). Effects of alternative training methods on self-efficacy and performance in computer software training. *Journal of applied psychology, 74*(6), 884.

[26] Herath, T., & Rao, H. R. (2009). Encouraging information security behaviors in organizations: Role of penalties, pressures and perceived effectiveness. *Decision Support Systems, 47*(2), 154-165.

[27] Johnston, A. C., & Warkentin, M. (2010). Fear appeals and information security behaviors: An empirical study. *Management Information Systems, 34*(3), 549-566.

[28] Lee, S. M., Lee, S. G., & Yoo, S. (2004). An integrative model of computer abuse based on social control and general deterrence theories. *Information & Management, 41*(6), 707-718.

[29] Lerouge, C., Newton, S., & Blanton, J. E. (2005). Exploring the systems analyst skill set: perceptions, preferences, age, and gender. *Journal of Computer Information Systems, 45*(3).

[30] Liang, H., & Xue, Y. (2009). Avoidance of information technology threats: a theoretical perspective. *MIS Quarterly, 33*(1), 71-90.

[31] Liang, H., & Xue, Y. (2010). Understanding security behaviors in personal computer usage: A threat avoidance perspective. *Journal of the association for information systems, 11*(7), 394-413.

[32] McCoy, C. (2010). Perceived self-efficacy and technology proficiency in undergraduate college students. *Computers & Education, 55*(4), 1614-1617.

[33] [33] Marakas, G. M., Yi, M. Y., & Johnson, R. D. (1998). The multilevel and multifaceted character of computer self-efficacy: Toward clarification of the construct and an integrative framework for research. *Information systems research, 9*(2), 126-163.

[34] Ng, B. Y., Kankanhalli, A., & Xu, Y. C. (2009). Studying users' computer security behavior: A health belief perspective. *Decision Support Systems, 46*(4), 815-825.

[35] NICCS (2015). National initiative for cybersecurity careers and studies. https://niccs.us-cert.gov/awareness/awareness-home

[36] Ozer, E. M., & Bandura, A. (1990). Mechanisms governing empowerment effects: a self-efficacy analysis. *Journal of personality and social psychology, 58*(3), 472.

[37] Potosky, D. (2002). A field study of computer efficacy beliefs as an outcome of training: the role of computer playfulness, computer knowledge, and performance during training. *Computers in Human behavior, 18*(3), 241-255.

[38] Privacy rights website. (http://www.privacyrights.org/data-breach, last visited May 4, 2016)

[39] Puhakainen, P., & Siponen, M. (2010). Improving employees' compliance through information systems security training: an action research study. *MIS Quarterly*, 757-778.

[40] Rank, J., Pace, V. L., & Frese, M. (2004). Three avenues for future research on creativity, innovation, and initiative. *Applied Psychology, 53*(4), 518-528.

[41] Rezgui, Y., & Marks, A. (2008). Information security awareness in higher education: An exploratory study. *Computers & Security, 27*(7), 241-253.

[42] Rhee, H., Kim, C., & Ryu, Y. U. (2009). Self-efficacy in information security: Its influence on end users' information security practice behavior. *Computers & Security, 28*(8), 816-826.

[43] SANS Institute. (2001) (https://www.sans.org/reading-room/whitepapers/vpns/weakest-link-human-factor-lessons-learned-german-wwii-enigma-cryptosystem-738, last visited May 4, 2016)

[44] [44] Siponen, M. T. (2000). A conceptual foundation for organizational information security awareness. *Information Management & Computer Security, 8*(1), 31-41.

[45] Sommestad, T., Hallberg, J., Lundholm, K., & Bengtsson, J. (2014). Variables influencing information security policy CC: A systematic review of quantitative studies. *Information Management & Computer Security, 22*(1), 42-75.

[46] Straub Jr, D. W. (1990). Effective IS security: An empirical study. *Information Systems Research, 1*(3), 255-276.

[47] Straub, D. W., & Welke, R. J. (1998). Coping with systems risk: security planning models for management decision making. *MIS Quarterly*, 441-469.

[48] Torkzadeh, G., & Lee, J. (2003). Measures of perceived end-user computing skills. *Information & Management, 40*(7), 607-615.

[49] Torkzadeh, G., & Van Dyke, T. P. (2002). Effects of training on Internet self-efficacy and computer user attitudes. *Computers in Human Behavior, 18*(5), 479-494.

[50] Torkzadeh, G., Chang, J. C. J., & Demirhan, D. (2006). A contingency model of computer and Internet self-efficacy. *Information & Management, 43*(4), 541-550.

[51] Torkzadeh, R., Pflughoeft, K., & Hall, L. (1999). Computer self-efficacy, training effectiveness and user attitudes: An empirical study. *Behaviour & Information Technology, 18*(4), 299-309.

[52] Udo, G. J., Bagchi, K. K., & Kirs, P. J. (2010). An assessment of customers' e-service quality perception, satisfaction and intention. *International Journal of Information Management, 30*(6), 481-492.

[53] Vishwanath, A., Herath, T., Chen, R., Wang, J., & Rao, H. R. (2011). Why do people get phished? testing individual differences in phishing vulnerability within an integrated, information processing model. *Decision Support Systems, 51*(3), 576-586.

[54] Witte, K. (1994). Fear control and danger control: A test of the extended parallel process model (EPPM). *Communications Monographs, 61*(2), 113-134.

Identity Theft Education: FIT Report

Susan Helser
shelser@norwich.edu

Computer Science, Computer Security
and Information Assurance

Norwich University
Northfield, Vermont

Abstract - Identity theft losses are in the billions of dollars. The crime affects individuals and industry. It consumes valuable resources and results in higher costs across the board. Technical strategies to address the problem have had mixed effects. The focus of this work is to report outcomes from research that assessed two distinct educational methods that targeted identity theft at the college level. One mode of presentation is text-based while the other is game-based. Study data show that students exposed to information through the game-based approach scored better on the identity theft assessment than did their counterparts who experienced the same information through the text-based method. Also, game-based participants remained longer in the educational unit and reported greater satisfaction than their text-based counterparts. Digital educational game-based learning is in its infancy. FIT demonstrates the efficacy of this method in the field of cyber education.

Categories and Subject Descriptors

[Software organization and properties]: *Virtual Worlds Software – Interactive Games*

[Human and Societal Aspects of Security and Privacy]: *Social Aspects of Security and Privacy*

[Human Computer Interaction (HCI)]: *HCI Design and Evaluation Methods-User Studies*

[Education]: *Interactive Learning Environments*

[Professional Topics]: *Computer Crime – Identity Theft*

General Terms

Identity Theft, Identity Theft Education, Text- and Game-Based Learning, Interactive Learning, Cyber Security

Keywords

Con, Cyber Crime, Deceive, Deception, Education, Fraudster, Identity, Identity Theft, Identity Thieves, Malware, Phishing, Personally Identifiable Information (PII), Scam, Steal, Theft

1 INTRODUCTION

Identity theft continues to grow and evolve at an alarming rate. Millions of people's lives have been affected. Unknown and unwarranted legal trouble haunts the victim, often years after the person's *identity* is stolen. Losses totaling in the hundreds of billions of dollars impact the consumer, business and the economy as a whole. The cost of fraudulently acquired goods and services are passed on from industries such as retail and the medical community to the public through higher prices and premiums.

Malware is one of the tools successfully used by *identity thieves* to steal *PII*, aka personally identifiable information. Figures 1 through 4 reflect the severity of the problem. They indicate the extent to which *malware* is used. The creators of the infectious code work diligently to design it in such a way that it is able to pass unnoticed. Without regular and substantive checks, electronic systems are susceptible. In recent years large retailers' billing technology has been targeted. Corrupted systems continued to process financial transactions, but passed on sensitive information to the remote *fraudster*. In addition to the loss of *PII*, events had a substantial and detrimental effect on the businesses [18, 27, 29, 36, 39, 41, 42]. Data displayed in Figures 1 through 6 is available from the *Anti-Phishing Working Group* (APWG) [1, 2, 3, 4, 5, 6, 7, 8].

The APWG collects and disseminates information that concerns *phishing* related cyber activities. Statistics are computed from self-reported events from individuals and companies. Figures 1 and 2 show *Malware by Strain* in 2015 and 2016. *Trojans* continue to represent a major concern. From their inception they are designed to be unseen. Figures 3 and 4 show the percent of *Malware Infections by Type* for the same two-year period. Similarly, *Trojans* constitute a significant form of attack. Their detection presents a real challenge. Figures 5 and 6 report the *Most Targeted Industries* for 2015 and 2016. Vulnerabilities exist and are readily exploited by *identity thieves*. Some industries such as financials are targeted, but no sector is immune. In addition to harm to the individual, economic losses are catastrophic [15, 16, 17, 23, 34, 25, 28, 30, 31, 32, 33]. Consequences are sufficient to undermine the economy [43, 44, 45, 46, 47, 48, 49].

Methods to address the crime of *identity theft* have been varied with mixed results. Technical and non-technical strategies have been tried. Technical solutions have limited effect, in part, because the problem involves people and their behavior. Educational resources that consist of informational text materials provided by numerous government and non-government agencies are available on Internet websites and in pamphlets. The message has reached some people, but more must be done to combat *identity theft*. Another strategy is needed, one that moves in a new direction to inform citizens of the ongoing threats posed by the *crime*. An engaging method to deliver critical and relevant material is crucial. For this reason, *Fight Identify Theft* (FIT) was developed. FIT is an educational *identity theft* game.

To assess FIT's value as an instructional tool this study compares results from exclusively text-based learning to a game-based approach. Because college students are targeted by *identity thieves* due to their increasing earning potential over time, the focus of this research is centered on this group. Study results reflect greater improvement between *identity theft* pre- and post-surveys, time participants remained in the educational module, and benefit and enjoyment responses for game-based learners than for their text-based counterparts. Results are reported in this paper.

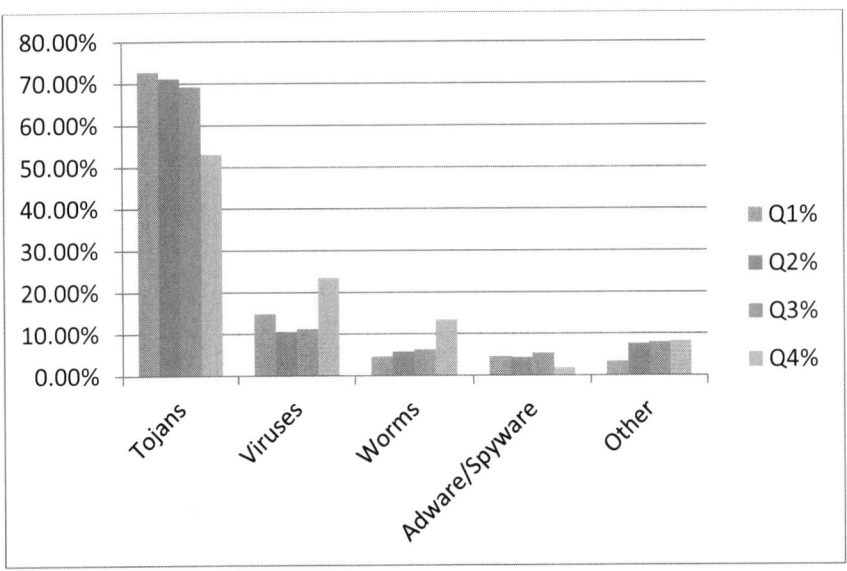

Figure 1: 2015 % Malware by Strain

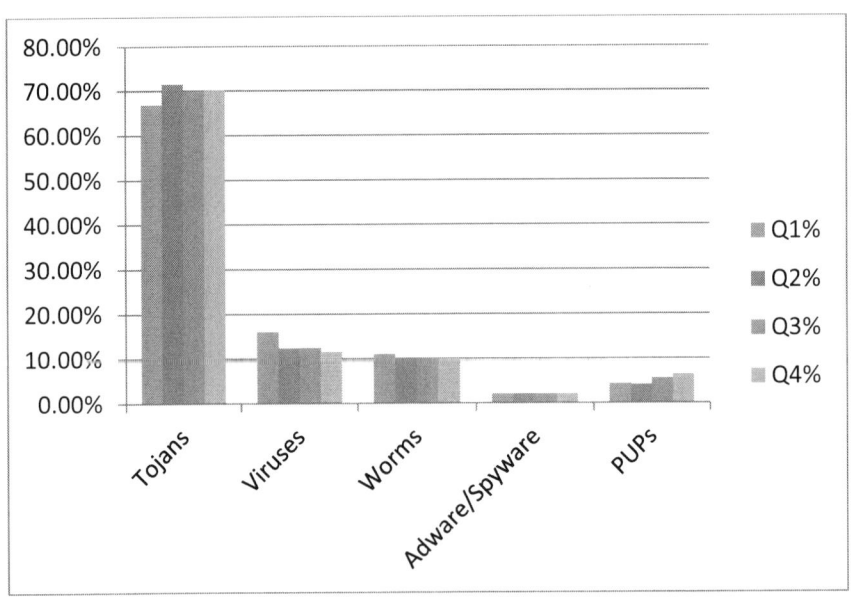

Figure 2: 2016 % Malware by Strain

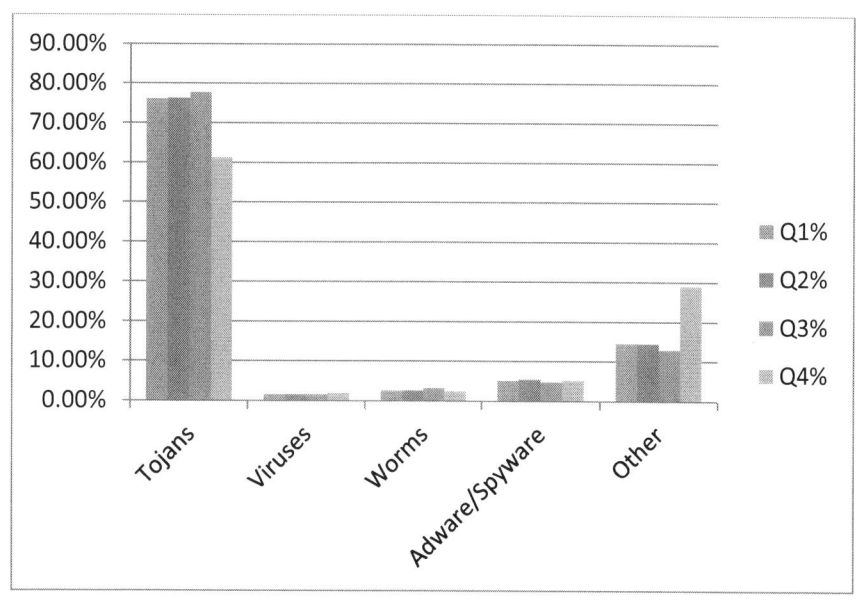

Figure 3: 2015 % New Malware Infections by Type

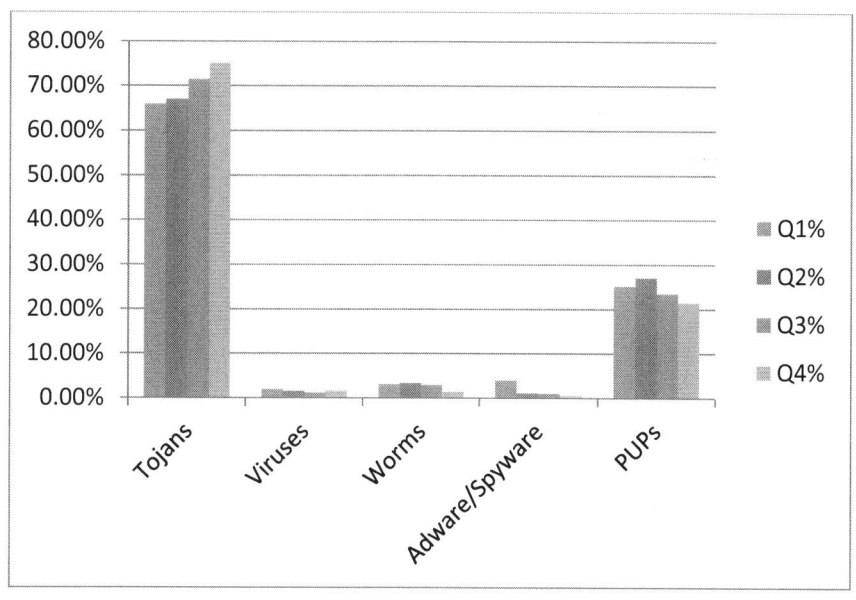

Figure 4: 2016 % Malware Infections by Type

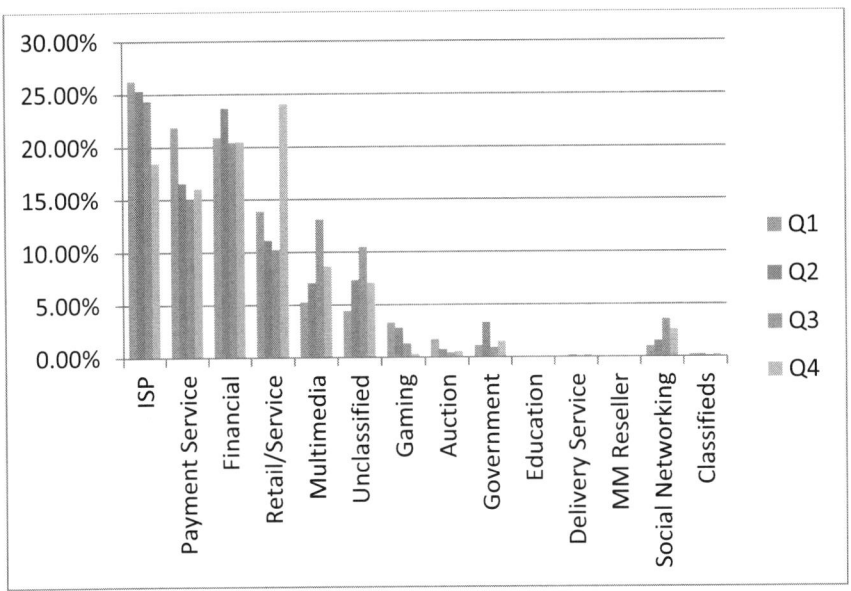

Figure 5: 2015 Most Targeted Industries

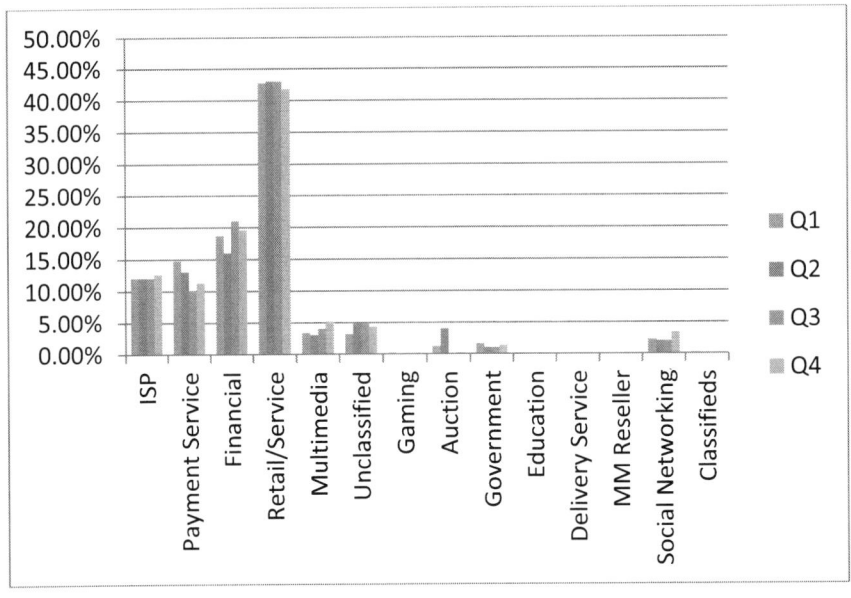

Figure 6: 2016 Most Targeted Industries

110

2   OBJECTIVE

The objective of this research is to assess the efficacy of game-based learning about *identity theft* in relation to a traditional text-based format that presents the same material to college students. Participants in the study are at least 18 years of age. *Fraudsters* exploit the population regardless of demographic information, because individuals' *identities* have value. Given the appropriate documentation, people are able to gain credit which, in turn, can be used by the actual person or by anyone who appears to be that individual. In the case of college students, the worth of their *identities* tends to grow with time as they proceed through their educational goals and careers. It is possible that an *identity thief* will retain a student's *identity* information for a number of years before reaping any benefit. The assumption is that upon completion of a college degree that the former student, now entering the workforce, will be able to access a significantly greater amount of credit. Given this scenario, it makes sense for a *fraudster* to be patient and to wait before using or selling the *identity*.

Currently, numerous printed resources that address *identity theft* are available [11, 20, 21, 34, 37,40]. Materials are useful and informative, but more needs to be done to reach a greater number of individuals. One possibility that is considered in this research is game-based learning [9, 10, 12, 13, 14, 19, 22, 26, 35, 38]. Because of the format, this method affords the opportunity to address different learning modalities. For example, rather than presenting information exclusively as text, audio and video components can be incorporated. Engaging digital resources can be created and then adapted to suit the respective educational requirements of a discipline. Data gathered from the assessment of the learning tool regarding what is effective can be used to make improvements and enhancements.

3   METHODOLOGY

To help educate college students about the *crime* of *identity theft* FIT was developed. It is a software application that incorporates game-based learning. To assess FIT's efficacy, two independent educational modules are used to present identical content, but through different means. One is a traditional text-based delivery system similar to what can be found on the Internet, in pamphlets or in periodicals. The other is a new game-based approach complete with scoring, colorful graphics, audio, video and puzzles. In addition, FIT includes the collection of demographic data, the administration of pre- and post- surveys used to assess participants' knowledge of *identity theft*, and three areas for users to supply feedback about their experience by way of enjoyment level, benefit level and open response. Time is recorded as well. Figure 7 shows FIT flow.

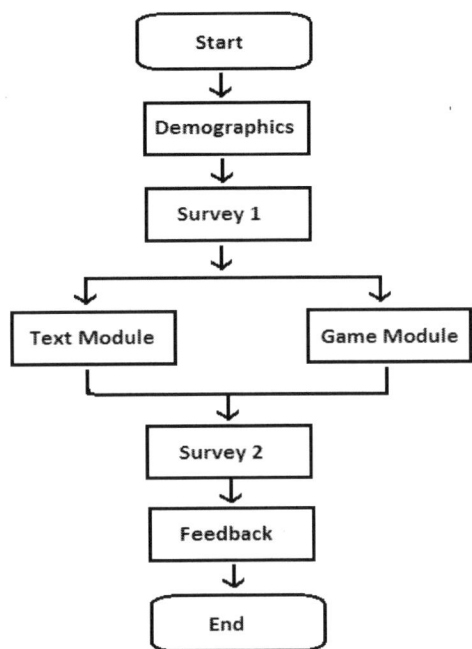

Figure 7: FIT Flowchart

After an individual agrees to participate and enters the requested demographic information he or she receives Survey 1, the first of a set of two identical survey questions that include the following:

1. Identity theft can lead to credit problems.

2. Medical insurance can be denied, because of identity theft.

3. It is smart to buy from the cheapest online vendor.

4. Phishing can occur at work.

5. Social engineering is a form of social media.

6. It's okay to stay logged on to a computer when you leave it for a few minutes.

7. Purchases that you don't make don't impact your credit.

8. Social media sites are good places to share your information.

9. Cell apps are reliable.

Once Survey 1 has been completed FIT randomly selects one of the two educational modules. The individual then has the opportunity to explore resources that are available in that particular unit. Topics include *finance, health, entertainment, work, home, education, shopping, home, and mobile communication.* In the case of the text-based track nine topic specific panels that include six paragraphs of material about different areas where PII is at risk can be viewed in any order. A participant is free to remain on a given panel, can leave the panel to select another topic area to investigate, or return to a previously viewed panel. Figures 8 – 10 show the selection screen for the text-based module and a sample of two text-based informational panels.

Figure 8: Text Screen

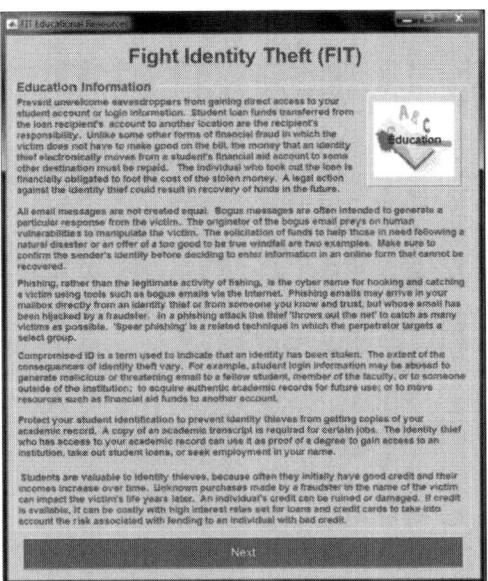

Figure 9: Education Text Panel

114

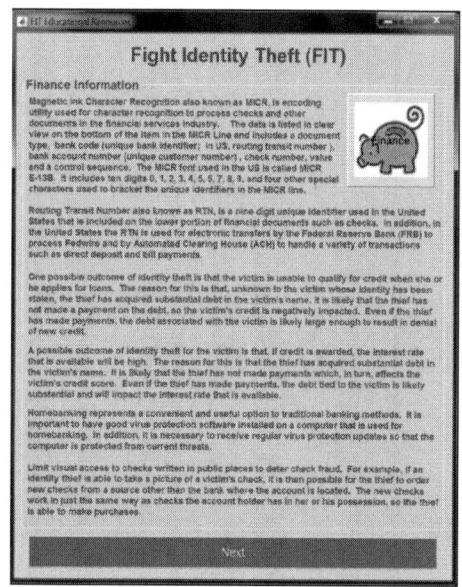

Figure 10: Finance Text Panel

The same material is presented in the game-based module, but through variety of formats. Nine colorful buttons used to select topics replace text-based panels. Similarly, sets of six game-panels with "clues" that address each of the nine topic areas are used. "Clues" correspond to paragraphs in the text-based unit. Three game panels are presented in a Q & A format. Content on these panels is identical to text that appears in the text-based module. Two of the three remaining game-based panels have "clues" in the form of messages that are either of audio of video format. Information is the same as what is displayed on the text-based panels, but delivered differently. Participants can access the audio or video resources repeatedly, so long as they remain on a particular game panel. The last of the six game panels includes a word search puzzle with terms that are related to the text "clue" on the screen. Figures 11 – 17 show the user selection screen and a sample of the game play panels.

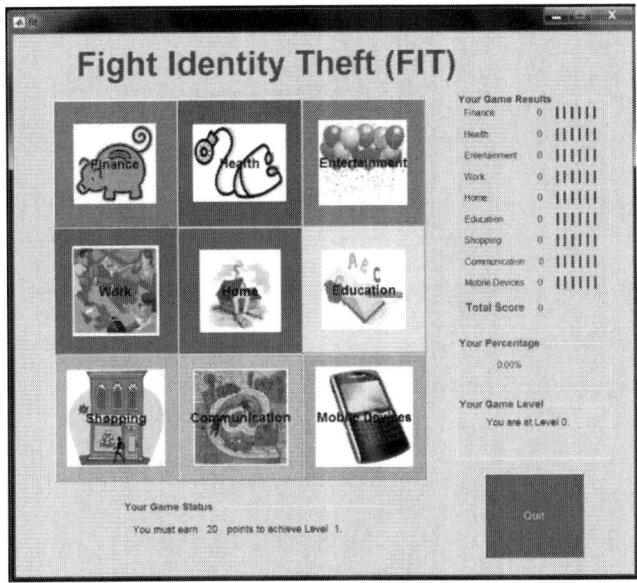

Figure 11: Game Screen

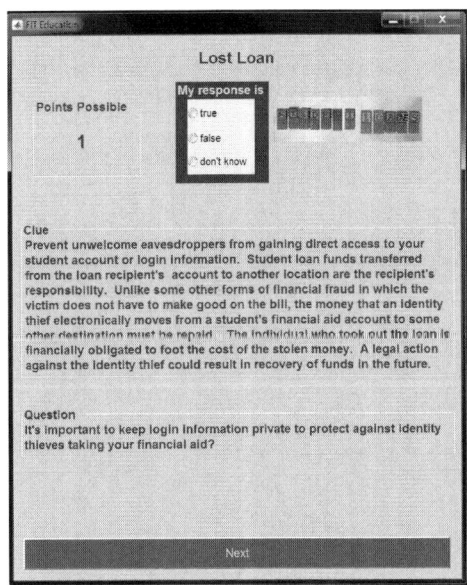

Figure 12: Lost Loan Game Panel

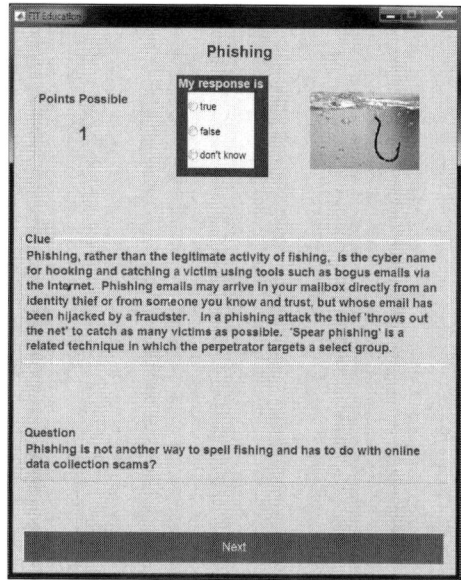

Figure 13: Phishing Game Panel

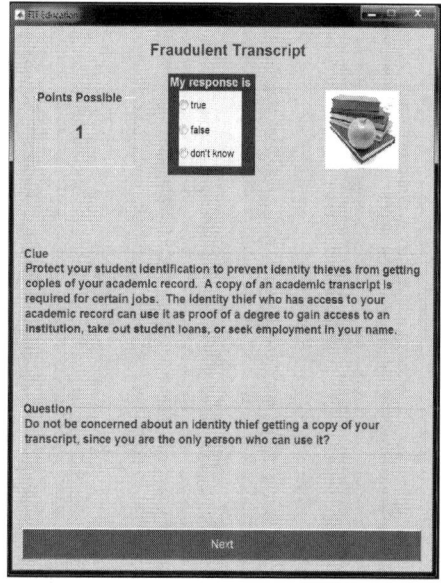

Figure 14: Fraudulent Transcript Game Panel

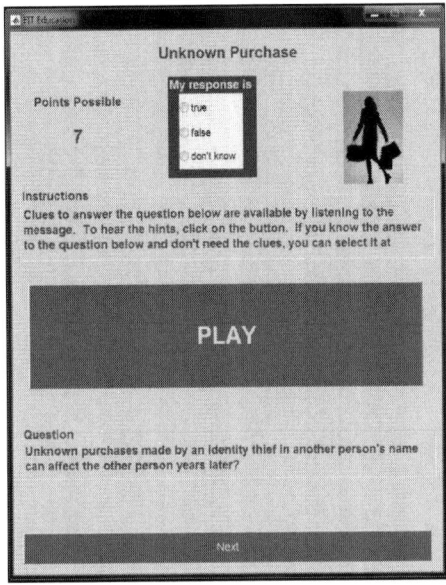

Figure 15: Unknown Purchase Game Panel

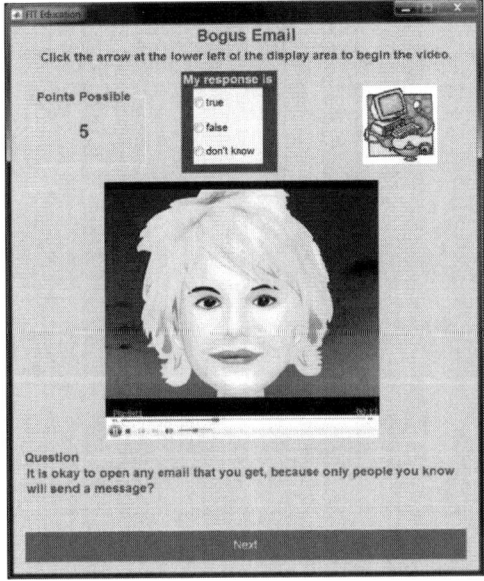

Figure 16: Bogus Email Game Panel

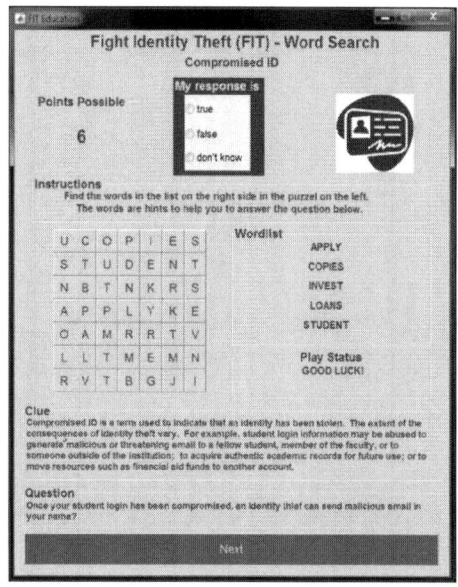

Figure 17: Word Search Game Panel

In the case of the game modules, points are awarded for correct responses. Questions are weighted differently so points earned vary. This is indicated in the Points Possible box that is displayed on each game panel screen. Users can view their status in the game anytime they return to the main screen. Statistics include the participant's score, relative percentage in the game, number of points needed to reach the next level, current level, and how many questions remain to be answered in a given topic area. Participants can exit the game module at any time.

After a participant quits either of the learning modules he or she receives Survey 2, second of the set of two identical surveys. Data collected in pre - and post - surveys for both groups is used to assess movement in the participant's responses to the survey questions. Three responses are possible that include *true*, *false* and *don't know*. Scoring for nine combinations of possibilities is listed in Table 1. The terms *incorrect*, *don't know*, and *correct* reflect whether a participant answered the question correctly. For example, suppose a participant indicates the *incorrect* response on Survey 1 and answers in the same way on Survey 2, then no points are awarded, since no change occurred. On the other hand, if the participant answered *don't know* on Survey 1, but responded the *correct* answer on Survey 2, then 1 point is awarded that reflects positive movement following the exposure to the educational module.

S1 vs. S2	incorrect	don't know	correct
incorrect	0	1	2
don't know	–1	0	1
correct	–2	–1	0

Table 1: Fit Score Scheme

Scores for each of the nine questions were determined in this way then added together for each participant. Figure 18 displays the results. Text-based results are displayed in blue while game-based results appear in red. The distribution of game-based data (red) is to the right of text-based data (blue). This reflects better performance on for game-based learners on the assessment.

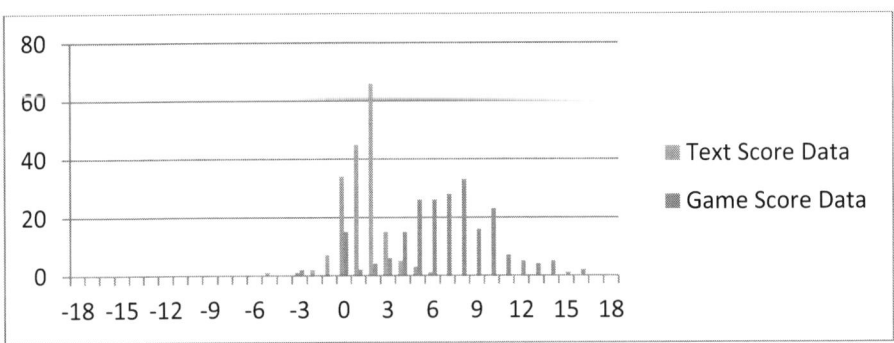

Figure 18: Game and Text Score Data

120

The total length of time an individual remains in the software is recorded. This in relation to the score received as described above is reported in Table 2. In addition, participants have the opportunity to supply feedback about their experience with FIT by way of benefit, enjoyment and in an open response area. Data for benefit and enjoyment are reported in Table 3.

	Text		Game	
	Score	Time	Score	Time
Average	1.36	527	6.85	1002
Std. Dev.	1.4	237	3.46	548
Minimum	-5	36	-3	40
Maximum	6	2373	16	4368
Correlation	0.24		-0.12	

Table 2: FIT Scores and Time

	Text		Game	
	Benefit	Enjoy	Benefit	Enjoy
Average	1.69	2.37	4.18	4.12
Std. Dev.	0.81	1.03	1.22	1.2
Minimum	1	1	1	1
Maximum	4	5	5	5

Table 3: Benefit and Enjoyment

4   SOFTWARE AND TECHNOLOGY

The Mathwork's software MATLAB was used to write FIT. The program was written on a PC platform using the MATLAB graphical user interface GUIDE. Microsoft images were used for the graphics on the numerous panels. Audio sound effects were selected from *6000 Sound Effects* from COSMI. CyberLink YouCam was used to produce the videos. Microsoft code was embedded in the MATLAB application to play the videos. The entire coding project required approximately one year.

5   RESULTS

F-table for $\alpha = 0.05$

(http://www.socr.ucla.edu/Applets.dir/F_Table.html)

$H_0: \delta_1^2 = \delta_2^2$ $\qquad\qquad$ $H_1: \delta_1^2 \neq \delta_2^2$

	Game (1)	Text (2)	F Score
n	220	180	
Degrees freedom	219	179	
Time (variance)	300772.44	56338.63	4.37
Score (variance)	11.96	1.97	4.96
Benefit (variance)	1.49	0.65	1.87
Enjoyment (variance)	1.45	1.06	1.12

Table 1: F-Test Results

t-table for $\alpha = 0.05$

(http://www.socr.ucla.edu/applets.dir/t-table.html)

$H_0: \mu_1 = \mu_2$ $\qquad\qquad$ $H_1: \mu_1 > \mu_2$

n1 = 220, n2 = 180 degrees freedom, n1 + n2 - 2 = 398	t	Critical Value
Time	11.58	1.645
Score	21.51	1.645
Benefit	24.42	1.645
Enjoyment	15.72	1.645

Table 2: t test

6   CONCLUSION

F- and t-test study results indicate the effectiveness of game-based learning to address *identity theft* education in college students. FIT scores and time spent learning about *identity theft* were greater for game-based participants. Feedback provided by the game-based learners was better for benefit and enjoyment levels. Open responses revealed greater satisfaction as well. Participants supplied a variety of suggestions to improve FIT. For example, participants recommended enhancing FIT to provide *resume* functionality so that a *player* could exit the game, return, and continue at a later time. Game-based players offered other ideas too, such as allowing *players* to revisit a question, even if it meant points earned would be reduced. Another suggestion was that participants be allowed to select questions to answer. Older students and those with young children asked that versions of FIT be written to educate the elderly and teens. A longitudinal study is another possibility. Additional work needs to be done.

REFERENCES

[1] Anti-Phishing Working Group, *Phishing Activity Trends Report 4th Quarter 2016*, http://docs.apwg.org/reports/apwg_trends_report_q4_2016.pdf

[2] Anti-Phishing Working Group, *Phishing Activity Trends Report 3rd Quarter 2016*, http://docs.apwg.org/reports/apwg_trends_report_q3_2016.pdf

[3] Anti-Phishing Working Group, *Phishing Activity Trends Report 2nd Quarter 2016*, http://docs.apwg.org/reports/apwg_trends_report_q2_2016.pdf

[4] Anti-Phishing Working Group, *Phishing Activity Trends Report 1st Quarter 2016*, http://docs.apwg.org/reports/apwg_trends_report_q1_2016.pdf

[5] Anti-Phishing Working Group, *Phishing Activity Trends Report 4th Quarter 2015*, http://docs.apwg.org/reports/apwg_trends_report_q4_2015.pdf

[6] Anti-Phishing Working Group, *Phishing Activity Trends Report 3rd Quarter 2015*, http://docs.apwg.org/reports/apwg_trends_report_q3_2015.pdf

[7] Anti-Phishing Working Group, *Phishing Activity Trends Report 2nd Quarter 2015*, http://docs.apwg.org/reports/apwg_trends_report_q2_2015.pdf

[8] Anti-Phishing Working Group, *Phishing Activity Trends Report 1st Quarter 2015*, http://docs.apwg.org/reports/apwg_trends_report_q1_2015.pdf

[9] S. A. Barab, M. Gresalfi, and A. Arici, *Why Educators Should Care About Games*, Educational Leadership, September 2009, Vol. 67, No. 1 pp 76 – 80.

[10] F. Bellotti, B. Kapralos, K. Lee, P. Moreno-Ger, and R. Berta, *Assessment in and of Serious Games: An Overview*, Hindawi Publishing Corporation, Advances in Human Computer Interaction, Vol. 2013, Article ID 136864, pp 1 – 11

[11] F. Cassim, *Protecting Personal Information in the Era of Identity Theft: Just How Safe is Our Personal Information from Identity Thieves?*, ISSN 1727-3781, PER: Potchefstroomse Elektroniese Regsblad, 18(2):pp 69 – 110, http://dx.doi.org/10.4314/pelj.v18i2.02, Retrieved March 14, 2017

[12] M-T Cheng, H-C She, and L.A. Annetta, *Game Immersion Experience: Its Hierarchical Structure and Impact on Game-based Science Learning*, Journal of Computer Assisted Learning, June 2015, Vol. 31 Issue 3, pp 232 – 253

[13] M. Csikszentmilhalyi, Applications of Flow in Human Development and Education, *Chapter 8: Intrinsic Motivation and Effective Teaching*, 2014 Springer Science & Business Media Dordrecht, DOI: 10.1007/978-94-017-9094-9_8, pp 173 – 187

[14] M. Csikszentmihalyi, *The Psychology of Optimal Experience*, Harper & Row; 1st Ed., March 1990, ASIN: B010EV0KHW

[15] *Deter, Detect, Defend, Avoid Theft*, https://www.in.gov/isp/files/Avoid_ID_Theft_Deter_Detect_Defend.pdf, Retrieved March 14, 2017

[16] *Expanding Service to Reach Victims of Identity Theft and Financial Fraud*, October 2010, http://www.ovc.gov/pubs/ID_theft/idtheftlaws.html, retrieved March 8, 2017

[17] Federal Trade Commission, August 27, 2014, *Can you spot a government imposter?*, Amy Hebert, https://www.consumerftc.gov/blog/whos-calling-not-government, retrieved February 18, 2017

[18] Federal Trade Commission, IdentityTheft.gov, https://identitytheft.gov/, retrieved February 16, 2017

[19] M. Gaydos, *Seriously Considering Design in Educational Games*, 2015, Educational Researcher, Vol. 44, No. 9, pp 478 – 483, DOI: 10.3102/0013189X15621307

[20] K. Higgins, *Price Tag Rises for Stolen Identities Sold in the Underground*, December 15, 2014, http://www.darkreading.com/attacks-breaches/price-tag-rises-for-stolen-identities-sold-in-the-underground/, retrieved February 27, 2017

[21] J. Hirschfeld Davis, *Hacking of Government Computers Exposed 21.5 Million People*, New York Times, July 9, 2015, http://www.nytimes.com/2015/07/10/us/office-of-personnel-management-hackers-got-data-of-millions.html, retrieved February 27, 2017

[22] M. A. Honey and M. Hilton, Editors, Learning Science Through Computer Games and Simulation, *Chapter 3: Simulation and Games in the Classroom*, pp 57 - 62, Chapter 7: Research Agenda for Simulation and Games, pp 119 – 128, National Academy of Science, ISB 978-0-309-38664-7, DOI: 10.17226/13078

[23] *Identity Protection: Prevention, Detection and Victim Assistance*, IRS, https://www.irs.gov/individuals/identity-protection, retrieved March 8, 2017

[24] *Identity Theft: Prevalence and Cost Appear to be Growing*, United States General Accounting Office, http://www.gao.gov/assets/240/233900.pdf, retrieved March 8, 2017

[25] Identity Theft Resource Center, June 24, 2013, http://www.idtheftcenter.org/Identity-Theft/how-much-is-your-identity-worth-on-the-black-market.html, retrieved March 18, 2017

[26] A. Iliya, A. Jabbar, and P. Felicia, *Gameplay Engagement and Learning Game-Based Learning: A Systematic Review*, Review of Educational Research, December 2015, Vol. 85, No. 4, pp 740 – 779, DOI: 10.3102/0034654315577210

[27] T. Judson MPH, M. Haas MBA, T Lagu MD MPH, *Medical Identity Theft: Prevention and Reconciliation Initiatives at Massachusetts General Hospital*, Joint Commission Journal on Quality & Patient Safety, July 2014, ; 40(7): pp 291 – 295

[28] D. Kirk, *Identifying Identity Theft*, The Journal of Criminal Law, 2014, DOI: 10.1177/0022018314557418, Vol. 78(6) pp 448 – 450

[29] Medicare.gov, *Help fight Medicare fraud*, https://www.medicare.gov/forms-help-and-resources/report-fraud-and-abuse/fraud-and-abuse.html, retrieved February 1, 2017

[30] A. C. Moise, *Identity Theft Committed Through the Internet*, Juridical Current, 2015, Vol. 18 Issue 2, pp 118 - 125

[31] T. Nagunwa, *Behind Identity Theft and Fraud in Cyberspace: The Current Landscape of Phishing Vectors*, International Journal of Cyber-Security and Digital Forensics. 3.1 (Jan. 2014): p72.

[32] *Phishing*, https://www.consumer.ftc.gov/articles/0003-phishing, retrieved February 1, 2017

[33] *Phone Scams*, August 6, 2016, https://www.consumer.ftc.gov/articles/0076-phone-scams, retrieved February 8, 2017

[34] Po-Ching Lin and Pei-Ying Lin, *Unintentional and involuntary personal information leakage on Facebook from user interactions*, KSII Transactions on Internet and Information Systems, July 2016, Vol. 10 Issue 7, pp 3301 – 3019

[35] L.P. Reiber, *Seriously Considering Play: Designing Interactive Learning Environments Based on the Blending of Microworlds, Simulations and Games*, 1996, ETR&D, Vol. 44, No. 2, pp 43 – 58, ISSN 1042-1629

[36] M. Riley, B. Elgin, D. Lawrence, C. Matlack, *Missed Alarms and 40 Million Stolen Credit Card Numbers: How Target Blew It*, Bloomberg News, March 17, 2015, http://www.bloomberg.com/news/articles/2014-03-13/target-missed-warnings-in-epic-hack-of-credit-card-data, retrieved February 6, 2017

[37] J. Showronski, *What Your Information is Worth on the Black Market*, http://www.bankrate.com/finance/credit/what-your-identity-is-worth-on-black-market.aspx, retrieved March 8, 2017

[38] V. J. Shute and F. Ke, Assessment in Game-Based Learning: Foundations, Innovations, and Perspectives, *Chapter 4 Games, Learning, and Assessment*, 2012 Springer Science & Business Media Dordrecht, pp 43 - 58, DOI: 10.1007/978-1-4614-3546-4_4

[39] *6 More Stores Attacked By Same Hack As Target: Firm*, Jim Finkle, January 25, 2014, http://www.huffingtonpost.com/2014/01/17/six-other-stores-are-bein_n_4618414.html, retrieved March 27, 2017

[40] L. Sweeney, *Data Privacy Lab SOS Social Security Number Watch*, IQSS Harvard University, http://dataprivacylab.org/projects/ssnwatch/index.html

[41] *Target: 40 Million Credit Card Compromised*, December 19, 2013, http://money.cnn.com/2013/12/18/news/companies/target-credit-card/index.html, retrieved March 27, 2017

[42] *Target Missed Signs of a Data Breach*, Elizabeth Harris and Nicole Perlroth, March 13, 2014, http://www.nytimes.com/2014/03/14/business/target-missed-signs-of-a-data-breach.html?_r=0, retrieved March 27, 2017

[43] *The Challenge of Health Care Fraud*, National Health Care Anti-Fraud Association, https://www.nhcaa.org/resources/health-care-anti-fraud-resources/the-challenge-of-health-care-fraud.aspx, retrieved April 2, 2017

[44] United States General Accountability Office, August 20, 2014, *Identity Theft Additional Actions Could Help IRS Combat the Large, Evolving Threat of Refund Fraud*, http://www.gao.gov/assets/670/665368.pdf, retrieved April 2, 2017

[45] United States General Accountability Office, May 24, 2016, *Identity Theft and Tax Fraud IRS Needs to Update Its Risk Assessment for the Taxpayer Protection Program*, http://www.gao.gov/assets/680/677406.pdf, retrieved April 8, 2017

[46] United States General Accountability Office, June 23, 2016, *Identity Theft Tax Refund Fraud*, http://www.gao.gov/multimedia/podcasts/677925, retrieved April 8, 2017

[47] United States General Accountability Office, November 29, 2012, *Identity Theft Total Extent of Refund Fraud Using Stolen Identities is Unknown*, http://www.gao.gov/assets/660/650365.pdf, retrieved April 18, 2017

[48] United States General Accountability Office, April 12, 2016, *Information Security IRS Needs to Further Improve Controls over Taxpayer Data and Continue to Combat Identity Theft Refund Fraud*, http://www.gao.gov/assets/680/676493.pdf, retrieved April 2, 2017

[49] United States General Accountability Office, April 19, 2016, *Tax Filing: IRS Needs a Comprehensive Customer Service Strategy and Needs to Better Combat Identity Theft Refund Fraud and Protect Taxpayer Data*, http://www.gao.gov/assets/680/676675.pdf, retrieved March 7, 2017

Journal of The Colloquium for Information System Security Education (CISSE)
Edition 5, Issue 1 - October 2017

Smart TV Upgrade, Privacy Downgrade?

Abdifatah Abdi-Nur
hirsi018@umn.edu

Michele Azar
ararx013@umn.edu

Chueyee Fang
fangx264@umn.edu

Cindy Hoffman
hoff0262@umn.edu

University of Minnesota Technological Leadership Institute
Distinguished Advisor - Dr. Faisal Kaleem
Minneapolis, MN U.S.A.

Abstract - The purpose of this paper is to create public awareness for privacy and to better protect consumers from Smart TV vulnerabilities. The analysis highlights many of the seemingly harmless Samsung preloaded applications that offer consumers little privacy. With the skyrocketing sales of Smart TVs, comes a critical challenge to protect customers' Personally Identifiable Information (PII). The need to educate and drive security awareness falls on both the private and public sector. Manufacturers, retailers, customers, and legislators need to help define the scope of protection required to mitigate the risk. This paper looks at the need to create public awareness for privacy and explore possible mitigation strategies to better serve and protect consumers from Smart TV vulnerabilities.

Categories and Subject Descriptors

K.3.2 [Computers and Education]: *Computer and Information Science Education*

General Terms

Privacy, Security

Keywords

CISSE, Education, IoT, Internet, Privacy, Regulation, Security, Smart Home, Television, TVs, University of Minnesota.

1   INTRODUCTION

There has been a rapid increase in Smart TV ownership and vulnerabilities. This accelerated growth began in December 2012 when news outlets reported that Smart TVs were the next untapped frontier for data theft [1]. Three years later, in February 2015, Samsung admits to spying on consumers by enabling the TV's microphone [2]. Moving forward to late 2015 and early 2016, a Symantec employee infects his TV with ransomware [3]. Most Smart TVs are shipped with default applications, such as Amazon, Hulu, and Netflix. That said, there are concerns over the details of what user information is sent and where it goes. When default applications were launched, and executed, several conversations to external entities occurred. Two important points were discovered during this analysis: 1) the chatter was not always specific to the launched application; and 2) the privacy agreement did not clarify what information was considered private. This paper covers data transmissions under the Obama administration and the Federal Communications Commission's legal authority to restrict manufacturers from a privacy free-for-all. However, there's been a change in elected officials with Donald Trump sworn in as the 45th president of the United State on January 20, 2017 [4]. Since the change in political office, President Trump signed a bill on April 4, 2017 repealing the Federal Trade Commission's authority to restrict consumer privacy and enable manufacturers to obtain and sell individual's data to the highest bidder [5]. It is imperative consumers learn and practice digital citizenship skills in order to navigate "the digital world safely, responsibly, and ethically" [6].

2 BACKGROUND

The Smart TV came into existence late 2005 as a method to standardize web content for Consumer Electronics (CE) devices [7]. The focus was to establish a way for consumers to have a lean-back Internet experience on CE devices without major effort by the content industry. This benchmark quickly accelerated into CE-HTML standard. In 2007, the Netherlands implemented a pilot program to test the market's appetite for the newly created Internet TV. The following year, Philips Electronics company matured the digital web technology and introduced the Smart TV as part of its LED TV collection in spring of 2009. This introduction was followed by an increase in production and became a magnet for content providers around the world who coined the new discovery as the "Smart TV" invention. Since 2009, the Smart TV industry has grown toward its current position with hundreds of applications available and a wide variety of Smart TV - enabled products including the Samsung brand which was tested in this paper.

2.1 A Smart TV is more powerful than a traditional TV

Not long ago, traditional TVs were used as a medium to watch news broadcasts, children's programming, and commercial shows and movies [8]. Families would make a point to be home in time to watch the latest miniseries or favorite programs. Today post-millennials, also known as Generation Z, are considered "first to have technology available at a young age" or said another way - bathed in bits [9]. This generation is accustomed to accessing media-on-demand and watching their favorite show while texting on their mobile device. The Smart TV is only one portion of the smart device sector. By the year 2009, the number of smart devices had surpassed the number of people on the planet [10]. This equates to 22.9 billion machines connected to the Internet [11]. The reason people should care about all these interconnected devices is that each device serves as a doorway for hackers to gain access to home or work networks. That said, while consumers may view their Smart TV as a medium for entertainment, Smart TVs actually pose a threat to the home - similar to a computer running out-of-date software that translates to known vulnerabilities.

3   APPROACH

The approach included the use of free open source software tools to discover abnormal traffic patterns and risky protocols destined to third parties. Software applications and devices utilized in this analysis included the following four components: 1) a network protocol analyzer tool (Wireshark 2.2.1) [12]; 2) Samsung Smart TV; 3) MacBook Air; and 4) a network capture investigator tool (Netwitness).

Samsung uses a Linux-based operating system named Tizen [13]. This architecture is an open-source software development system utilized by several different types of devices, such as, smartphones, tablets, home appliances and fitness trackers [14]. The outcome of utilizing the same software platform across several types is devices it to create a user-friendly and seamless user experience. Samsung's Tizen architecture. See Figure 1.

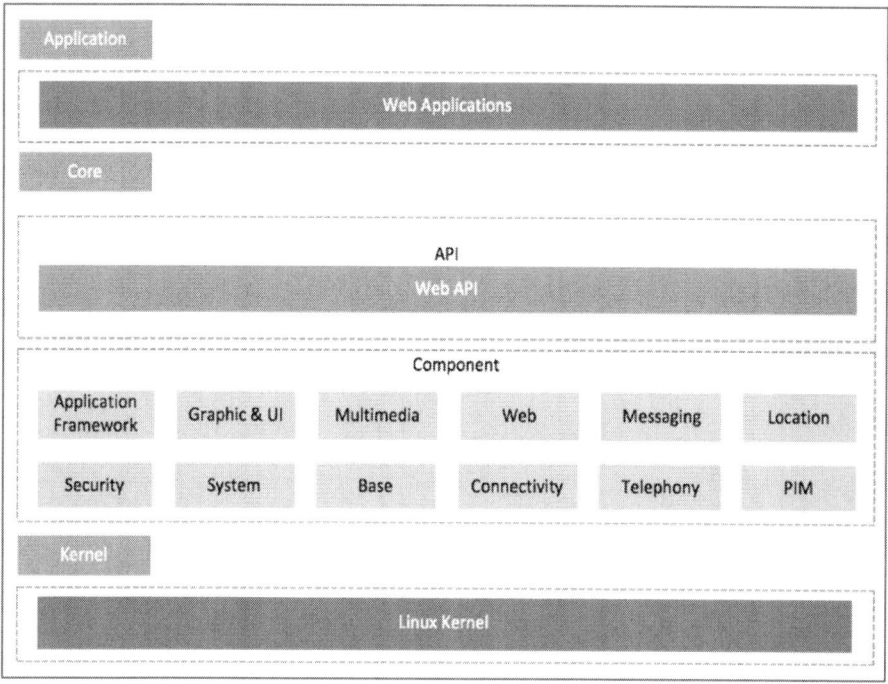

Figure 1: Tizen Operating System [14]

Our goal was to capture traffic between the Smart TV and Internet by examining six popular applications - Amazon Prime Video, Netflix, Hulu, YouTube, Fandango, and HBO GO preloaded by the manufacturer. The analysis was performed using Wireshark Version 2.2.1 to monitor wireless traffic sent between the Smart TV and the Internet as each preloaded application was individually launched. After the wireless traffic had completed for each default application, the traffic analysis was imported into a Netwitness software program to analyze each capture or log for inspection. The benefit of using Netwitness to examine packet captures was that Netwitness provides a detailed map of data as it travels between the application and the internet; whereas, Wireshark provides only a list of data transmitted between the Smart TV and the internet but does not include a way to filter or analyze the log.

4   ANALYSIS

The packet captures (.pcap files) taken from Wireshark were imported into Netwitness; which allowed us to narrow down the conversations between the Samsung Smart TV and the public internet to prove that information was being sent to third parties. It is unclear whether this information was used for malicious intent or to enhance the user experience.

4.1 Distinct exploit techniques utilize different skills and technologies

Smart TVs are vulnerable to Man-in-the-Middle (MitM) Attacks. MitM attacks likely occur in the following three user scenarios: 1) connecting to an OPEN network; 2) receiving application updates through non-secure sites; or 3) visiting an unsecure site through an application browser [15]. Intercepting wireless traffic with an open source network analyzer (Wireshark) as known as "sniffer" was simple. Even on a secured wireless network, the Smart TV was seen using a peer-to-peer protocol for screen mirroring; this is a default feature which means it is enabled right out of the box. Peer-to-Peer networking is dangerous because it can rapidly spread infected malware horizontally from one device to another without detection. Data captured in our analysis included clear text of the information shown in Figure 2 and appeared to be destined to a server located in Korea with the IP address: <http://www.sec.co.kr/dlna>.

Information shown in clear text:

- **Smart TV's Make/Model:** Samsung, LED 48 size screen

- **Model Name:** UN48J5200

- **Model Number:** 1.0

- **Screen Resolution:** 1920 x 1080

- **Serial Number:** 20090804RCR

- **UUID:** 08f0d180-0096-1000-bf66-fcf136df320e

Figure 2: Samsung TV Make/Model, SN, UUID and Screen Resolution details

Smart TVs are susceptible to Ransomware attacks where an attacker could install malicious code via the web; installing an infected application through a website redirects the information to a non-SSL site, local install (with a USB) or remote access management protocol (such as telnet and SSH) [16]. Tools like the SamyGO firmware patcher demonstrate how easy it is to enable remote management tools for potential malicious intent.

Summary Steps to Enable Telnet on Smart TV [17]

1. Download Firmware (i.e. T-CHU7DEUC.exe)file for your TV and unpack

2. Unpack it wine, unrar or pZip

3. Decrypt exe.img.enc in the T-CHU7DEUC/image directory using xor decryptor with key of firmware filename. Rename exe.img

4. Change contents of the rc.local in the decrypted exe.img file

5. Recalculate the CRC32 checksum and update the validinfo.xt

6. Update T-CHU7DEUC/image directory with new CRC information

7. Encrypt exe.img using xor encryption and copy into T-CHU7DEUC/image directory. Rename to exe.img.enc

8. Flash to TV with USB following firmware wizard

List of Components shown in Figure 3:

- Samsung LED 48 Smart TV model UN48J5200

- MacBook air running OS X Yosemite version 10.10.5

- Comcast Wireless Modem/Router

- Wireshark Network Protocol Analyzer version 2.2.1

- RSA Netwitness Investigator

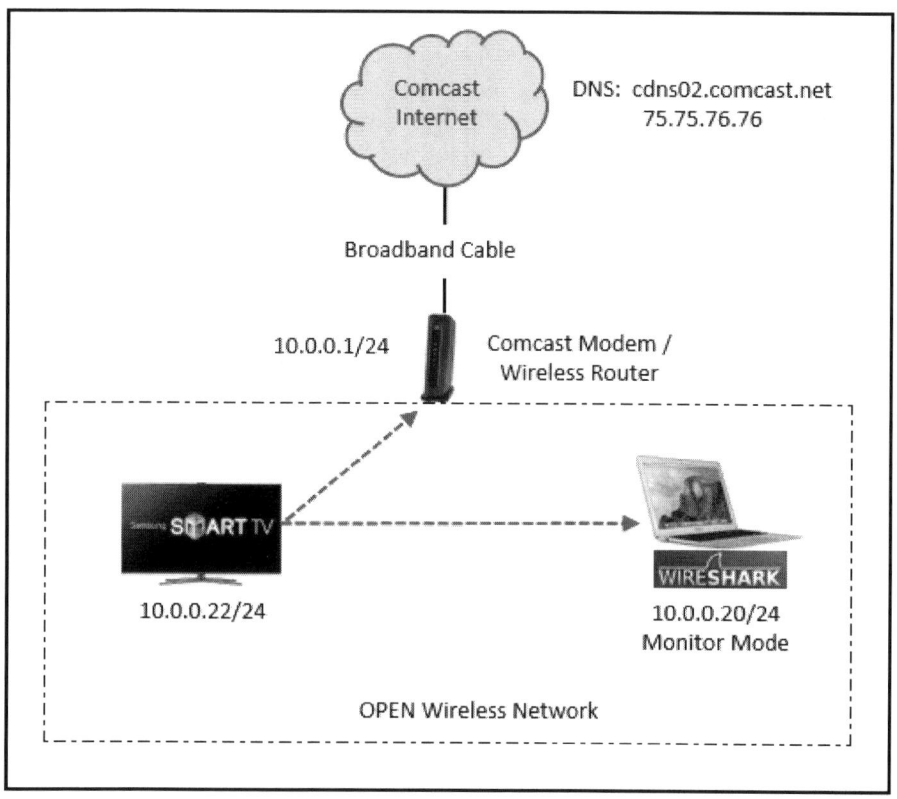

Figure 3: Network Diagram

Samsung Preloaded Applications:

- Amazon Prime Video

- Netflix

- Hulu

- YouTube

- Fandango

- HBO GO

From the analysis, it is highly likely that there were conversations to third party applications. Specifically, services hosted by Amazon AWS - 52.40.47.226 ec2-52-40-47-226.us-west-2.compute.amazonaws.com sent queries back to Navy Network Information Center (NNIC) - Virginia Beach domain name navy.mil, DoD Network Information Center – Nashville domain name army.mil, and the Commonwealth Scientific and Industrial Research Organization (CSIRO). Also, Figure 4 shows noticeable communications routed to China and the Russian Federation. Packets sent to these countries were encrypted; the data was not seen in clear text.

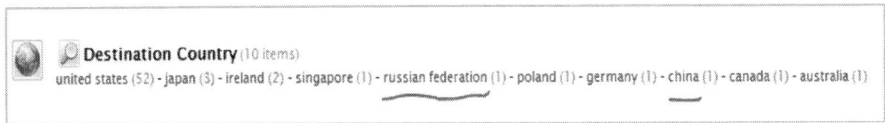

Figure 4: Amazon AWS communications sent to the U.S. and outside the U.S.

Several preloaded apps queried the applications website via non-Secure Socket Layer (SSL). The non-SSL website was eventually redirected to a secure SSL website; however, Figure 5, some of the preloaded apps like Fandango pulled images from non-SSL sites where the images were seen unencrypted and clearly visible.

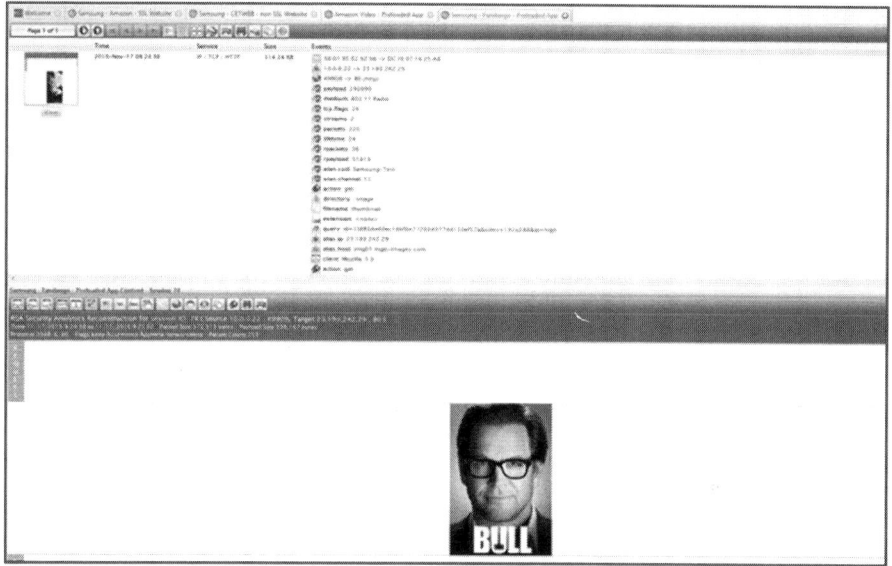

Figure 5: Fandango image from non-SSL site

To further support the analysis, additional testing was conducted to discover if traffic patterns were the same without launching any applications. From the discovery using Netwitness there were no risky protocols observed nor were there any queries to third party entities. The only traffic observed was to legitimate Samsung sites shown in Figure 6. Samsung websites shown in the screen capture include the following:

- <log-ingestion.samsungacr.com>

- <samsungcloudsolution.com>

- <upu.samsungelectronics.com>

- <noticeprd.cloudapp.net>

- <noticedn.samsungcloudsolution.com>

- <notice.samsungcloudsolution.com>

- <dpu.samsungelectronics.com>

139

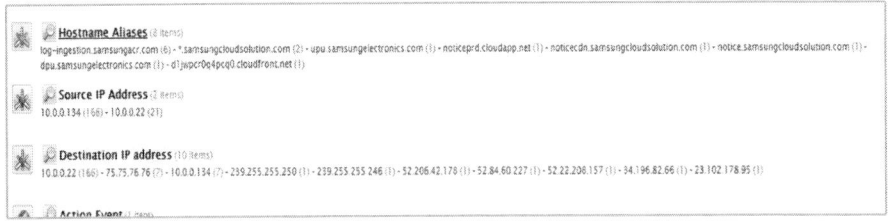

Figure 6: Traffic captures without any applications launched

Additional testing was performed in an attempt to capture usernames and passwords in clear text when logging into external sites like yahoomail.com and amazon.com. Since both yahoo mail and amazon use SSL for tunneling and data encryption, the captured packets did not reveal usernames and password information in clear text. An interesting outcome from this analysis, was the use of higher-level port numbers in all Netwitness reports. Higher level port numbers can be used by an attacker to open ports for remote access or backdoors and can also serve as a pathway for a hacker to deliver malware. In this example, the use of higher ports numbers is used to open a temporary data connection between the client and server for a specific service such as accessing the amazon application. Higher port numbers are also known as ephemeral or uncommon port number assignments. Figure 7 shows port numbers ranging from the commonly used port 80 up to less common port number of 55226.

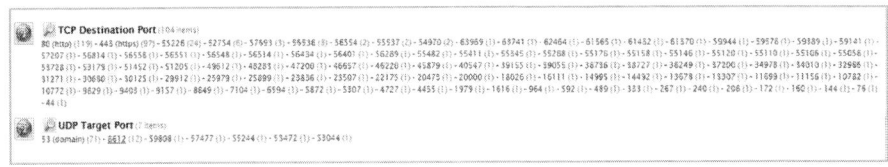

Figure 7: Destination ports used between external sites and Smart TV

5 THREAT ASSESSMENT / VULNERABILITY

For context, there are more devices connected to the Internet than there are people on the planet. This equates to 7.2 billion people worldwide with 25 billion devices for an average of 3.47 connected devices per person [10]. This is not necessarily a problem until hackers start exploiting these devices to gain access to home or work networks. Therefore, the risks of Smart TVs should not be understated. Smart TVs that connect to home or work networks often times contain out of date software and known vulnerabilities.

The television is the latest in a long line of devices to receive "smart" enhancements which make them operate like a computer rather than a display device. Smart TVs offer consumers web browser capabilities, increased network support and enhanced user convenience; however, unbeknownst to the consumer, Smart TVs introduce potential security vulnerabilities. There are three ways a hacker might infiltrate a home television: 1) through a JavaScript / HTML flaw, 2) through a Man-in-the-Middle attack or 3) IoT's expanded attack surface.

5.1 JavaScript / HTML flaws

All Smart TVs sold today, regardless of their underlying operating system, can run JavaScript and/or HTML. This should not be a surprise, "as compatibility with such standards is necessary for any modern device that wants to serve as a portal to the Internet. Unfortunately, these standards are vulnerable to attack," which arguably hasn't been widely understood by the public and private sectors [18]. Researchers SeungJin Lee and Seungjoo Kim, demonstrated a variety of attacks against the Samsung TV's operating system at the Black Hat USA 2013 conference [19]. These attacks included stealing a local user credentials, reading consumer's browser history and infiltrating the TV's built-in application architecture so that the system would crash; this wasn't the first report. In 2012, another pair of researchers "posted a video showing they had learned to remotely take control of a Samsung television," but the researchers failed to unveil their method [18].

Smart TV devices are vulnerable to many of the issues that haunt android systems. Google's operating system is the most targeted mobile Operating

System (OS) in the world, which means there's no shortage of malware for users to avoid. Threats range from simple advertising (ad) injectors that plague users with unwanted content to full-blown Trojans that can track browsing habits and log every move including passwords entered through Smart TVs.

5.2 The Man in the Middle

Hybrid Broadcast Broadband (HBB) is a popular standard for television because it is user-friendly. Customers can view previously played programs, take interactive content polls and shop on the Internet. In short, HBB is an emerging market worldwide with the highest rate of adoption being in Europe. However, the problem with HBB transmission is that they do not require a verified origin, which makes Smart TVs vulnerable to man-in-the-middle attacks [8]. To deploy this attack, a hacker would inject a malicious data packet via HBB's over-the-air transmission signal to infect the user's Smart TV or other devices connected to the same network.

5.3 IoT additions expand the threat landscape

Each "Smart" device that goes online open another path for hackers to infiltrate business and home networks. As noted in Europol's 2014 Threat Assessment with more objects begin connected to the Internet and the creation of new types of critical infrastructure, we can expect to see (more) targeted attacks on existing and emerging infrastructures, including new forms of blackmailing and extortion schemes (e.g., ransomware for smart cars or smart homes), data theft, physical injury and possible death, and new types of botnets'' [20] In the words of Chairman and Former CEO of Cisco, "it's no longer a question of if you'll be breached, it's a question of when" [21].

6 ACTIONABLE STEPS TO INCREASE THE SECURITY OF YOUR SMART TV

As the number of IoT devices increase, there are ways consumers can protect against attacks to the privacy of their Smart Home gadgets and personal network

[22]. Similar to locking a car or front door to a house to protect valuables, smart device security awareness and education must be added to that list. Table 1 outlines twelve steps all users can implement within their home network architecture to safeguard them from malicious attacks. Users who are more technically savvy, can go a step further and Segment normal "user" traffic from your Smart TV by creating separate VLAN (Virtual Local Area Networks). The hope is to have manufacturers and legislators work together to provide and promote the education of technical devices the same way physical security measures are publicized.

12 Ways to Increase the Security of Your Smart TV	
1	**Inventory Devices** Inventory all devices within your network. Disable or remove devices that are unknown or no longer used.
2	**Direct Connect** If possible, plug your TV directly to your Ethernet connection.
3	**Router Settings** If you choose to connect your TV to your home network: ■ Use a router with an enabled firewall ■ Hide your SSID ■ Select a secure password
4	**Automatic Updates** Set your TV to automatically update its software. Double-check to ensure that you have the latest update.

	12 Ways to Increase the Security of Your Smart TV
5	**Enable Smart Security Options on Samsung TVs** This is a new and critical option, available for the open source operating system (Tizen) which may pose more risk than other operating Systems.
6	**Careful What You Say or Do in Front of your TV** Cover the webcam and disable voice-activated controls.
7	**Limit Web Browsing** Keep web browsing to a minimum and <u>do not</u> perform banking activities from your Smart TV. Use your home computer or mobile device.
8	**Disconnect from the Internet** If you don't use its online features or are away for an extended length of time.
9	**Screen Mirroring Feature** Caution when using the screen mirroring feature, because your TV communicates with your nearby devices and may spread malware to all items within your home network.
10	**Limit Use of the Remote Management Technical Support Option** Remote management is used for technical support and by default should be disabled. If this option is enabled, it could leave your TV vulnerable to malware.

12 Ways to Increase the Security of Your Smart TV	
11	**Raise Public Awareness on IoT Crime Prevention & Safety Tips** Public awareness through community and local government websites for citizens to conveniently access; start youth programs to teach digital literacy where students can earn certificates or badges.
12	**Private Sector and Public-Sector Partnerships** Establish new partnerships to promote consumers from potential exploits of personal or financial data accessible through their Smart TV; an ideal partnership would be for Manufacturers to issue mandatory password change from its default setting on all devices
♀	**Create a Separate Network for your Smart TV** Segment normal "user" traffic from your Smart TV by creating separate VLAN (Virtual Local Area Networks).

Table 1: 12 Ways to Increase the Security of Your Smart TV

Digital Citizenship must be taught now and not further down the road as a reaction to loss of privacy and security. Furthermore, in addition to cyber awareness, digital literacy curriculums must be created and taught to children starting in kindergarten and to not only focus on middle and high school students [23]. There should be free Cyber Security events such as the one offered yearly at Metro State University in St. Paul, Minnesota each October [24]. Activities include workshops on internet and social media safety, computer and mobile device maintenance and education, how to secure your home network and electronic devices. IoT devices like the Smart TV should be included as part of the event curriculum [25]. These events provide local citizens with the tools necessary for cyber security while providing a no-cost option to individuals who may not be able to afford this expense because "attackers know no age' [23].

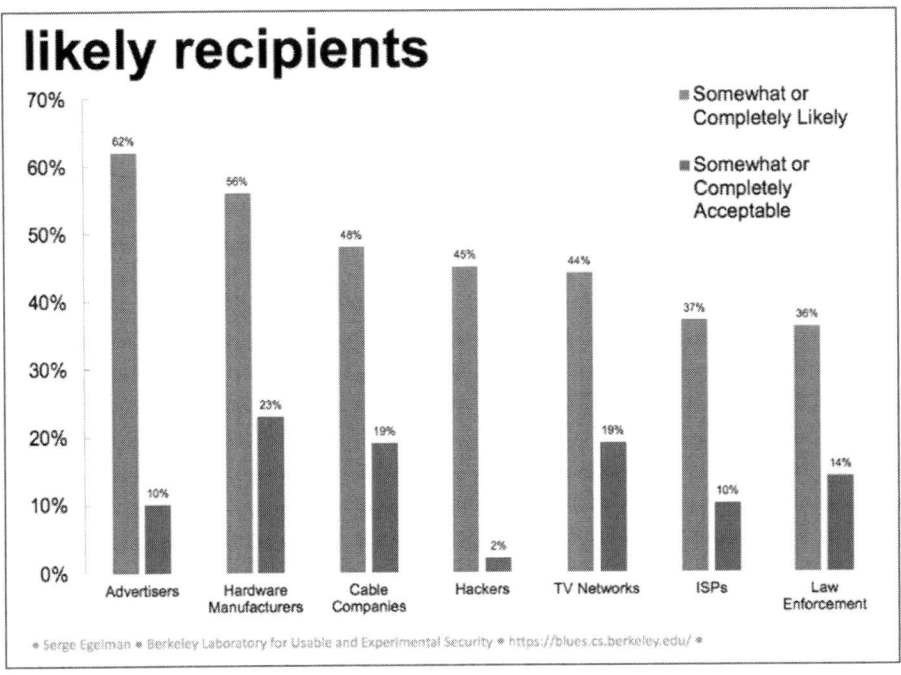

Figure 8: Survey to Gauge Comprehension of Risks Pertaining to Smart TV Data Capture

7   CONCLUSION

In conclusion, CE manufacturers and retailers alike forecast exponential growth in interconnected devices within the next few years; furthermore, the bullish projections of TVs connected to the internet will soar to 319 million by the year 2020 [26]. The next source of attacks will occur on consumers' Smart TVs. This paper underscores the need to heighten the awareness on Smart TV privacy concerns; specifically, there's a need to be more transparent with what information is disclosed without the user's knowledge and what precautionary steps need to be taken before agreeing to the Smart TV terms and conditions. Albeit small strides forward, these proactive steps serve as a way to help consumers enjoy their new Smart TVs and mitigate potential consumer privacy concerns or vulnerabilities to cyber exploits. In light of the recent announcement in which "VIZIO has agreed to pay $2.2 Million (to the Federal Trade Commission (FTC) and the State of New Jersey) as part of a settlement because VIZIO collected viewing histories on 11 million Smart TVs without users' consent" [27]. Table II shows the likely recipients who may obtain data from their Smart TV and whether or not it is "somewhat or completely acceptable" for advertisers, manufacturers, cable companies, hackers, networks, ISP and law enforcement to use that information [28]. "Many people incorrectly believe privacy laws prevent certain uses of their data. Others understand that the data can be shared, are opposed to it, but do not believe they can do anything about it" [28]. The need to educate and drive security literacy and awareness falls on both the private and public sector. Manufacturers, retailers, customers, and legislators need to help define the scope of protection required to mitigate the risk.

8 ACKNOWLEDGEMENT

The authors would like to thank our distinguished advisor, Dr. Faisal Kaleem for his guidance and expertise throughout this project. We would also like to thank the Technology Leadership Institute's faculty and board members at the University of Minnesota for the opportunity to contribute towards the success of bridging the gap between business and technology.

REFERENCES

[1] R. Wong, "Samsung Smart TVs: The next frontier for data theft and hacking [video]," a4 December 2012. [Online]. Available: http://bgr.com/2012/12/14/samsung-smart-tv-hack-security-exploit-discovered/. [Accessed 14 December 2016].

[2] M. Kumar, "The Hacker News," 8 February 2015. [Online]. Available: http://thehackernews.com/2015/02/smart-tv-spying.html. [Accessed 14 December 2016].

[3] C. Wueest, "How my TV got infected with ransomware and what you can learn from it," Symantec Security Response, 24 November 2015. [Online]. Available: https://www.symantec.com/connect/blogs/how-my-tv-got-infected-ransomware-and-what-you-can-learn-it. [Accessed 14 December 2016].

[4] New York Times, "Trump Sworn In as President," 20 January 2017. [Online]. Available: https://www.nytimes.com/video/us/politics/100000004863329/trump-swearing-in-ceremony-2017.html. [Accessed 23 April 2017].

[5] H. Neidig, "Trump signs internet privacy repeal," 3 April 2017. [Online]. Available: http://thehill.com/homenews/administration/327107-trump-signs-internet-privacy-repeal. [Accessed 22 April 2017].

[6] Common Sense Media, "Common Sense Media EdTech Glossary," [Online]. Available: https://www.commonsensemedia.org/educators/1to1/glossary. [Accessed 23 April 2017].

[7] Consumer Technology Association, "Consumer Technology Association - About Us," [Online]. Available: http://www.ces.tech/about-us. [Accessed 22 April 2017].

[8] M. Niemietz, J. Somorovsky, C. Mainka and J. Schwenk, "Not so smart: On Smart TV Apps," in International Workshop on Secure Internet of Things (SIoT), Vienna, 2015.

[9] Wikipedia, "Generation Z --- Wikipedia{,} The Free Encyclopedia," [Online]. Available: https://en.wikipedia.org/w/index.php?title=Generation_Z&oldid=764662907. [Accessed 11 February 2017].

[10] Evans, Dave; Cisco Internet Business Solutions Group (IBSG), "The Internet of Things: How the Next Evolution of the Internet is Changing Everything," Cisco, San Jose, 2011.

[11] Statista, "Statista - Internet of Things (IoT): number of connected devices worldwide from 2012 to 2020 (in billions)," [Online]. Available: https://www.statista.com/statistics/471264/iot-number-of-connected-devices-worldwide/. [Accessed 10 February 2017].

[12] Wireshark, "Wireshark 2.2.1 Release Notes," [Online]. Available: https://www.wireshark.org/docs/relnotes/wireshark-2.2.1.html. [Accessed 22 April 2017].

[13] Wikipedia contributors, "List of smart TV platforms and middleware software," 16 April 2017. [Online]. Available: https://en.wikipedia.org/wiki/List_of_smart_TV_platforms_and_middleware_sof tware. [Accessed 22 April 2017].

[14] International Institute of Cyber Security, "International Institute of Cyber Security - How to Hack your Smart TV," [Online]. Available: https://iicybersecurity.wordpress.com/2015/07/07/how-to-easily-hack-your-smart-tv-samsung-and-lg/. [Accessed 22 April 2017].

[15] N. Sidiropoulos and P. Stefopoulos, "Smart TV Hacking," University of Amsterdam, Amsterdam, 2013.

[16] M.-A. Russon, "International Business Times UK," 12 January 2016. [Online]. Available: http://www.ibtimes.co.uk/its-official-your-smart-tv-can-be-hijacked-malware-holding-viewers-ransom-1537533. [Accessed 14 December 2016].

[17] SamyGO Wiki, "How to enable Telnet on samsung TV's," [Online]. Available: https://wiki.samygo.tv/index.php?title=How_to_enable_Telnet_on_samsung_T V%27s. [Accessed 15 February 2016].

[18] J. Lee, "Make Use Of," 24 May 2014. [Online]. Available: http://www.makeuseof.com/tag/smart-tvs-are-a-growing-security-risk-how-do-you-deal-with-this/. [Accessed 14 December 2016].

[19] S. Lee and S. Kim, "Hacking, Surveilling, and Deceiving Victims on Smart TV," in Black Hat USA, Las Vegas, 2013.

[20] European Cybercrime Centre (EC3), "The Internet Organised Crime Threat Assessment (iOCTA)," European Police Office, 2014.

[21] Cisco, "Cisco Advanced Malware Protection Solution Overview," 3 January 2017. [Online]. Available: http://www.cisco.com/c/en/us/solutions/collateral/enterprise-networks/advanced-malware-protection/solution-overview-c22-734228.html. [Accessed 22 April 2017].

[22] S. Tiongco, "Tech Times," 20 June 2016. [Online]. Available: http://www.techtimes.com/articles/165859/20160620/how-to-protect-your-smart-tv-from-hackers-here-are-some-tips.htm. [Accessed 14 December 2016].

[23] M. Patane, "ISU rolls out cybersecurity curriculum for Iowa schools," 25 April 2015. [Online]. Available: http://www.desmoinesregister.com/story/tech/2015/04/26/isu-cybersecurity-curriculum/26282593/. [Accessed 23 April 2017].

[24] Metropolitan State University, "Think Safe, Be Safe: Cyber Security Awareness Month event," 22 October 2016. [Online]. Available: http://www.metrostate.edu/events/old-events/2016/october-2016/think-safe-be-safe-10-22-16. [Accessed 22 April 2017].

[25] Metropolitan State University, "Think Safe. Be Safe, Conference Agenda," 22 October 2016. [Online]. Available: https://metrocatalyst.files.wordpress.com/2016/10/conference_agenda-public.pdf. [Accessed 22 April 2017].

[26] The Digital TV Consultancy, "Connected TV set boom continues," 2016. [Online]. Available: http://www.digitaltvnews.net/?p=26270. [Accessed 15 December 2016].

[27] Federal Trade Commission, "VIZIO to Pay $2.2 Million to FTC, State of New Jersey to Settle Charges It Collected Viewing Histories on 11 Million Smart Televisions without Users' Consent," 6 February 2017. [Online]. Available: https://www.ftc.gov/news-events/press-releases/2017/02/vizio-pay-22-million-ftc-state-new-jersey-settle-charges-it. [Accessed 6 February 2017].

[28] Egelman, Serge - Berkeley Laboratory for Usable and Experimental Security, "Privacy perceptions surrounding smart TVs," 7 December 2017. [Online]. Available: https://www.ftc.gov/system/files/documents/public_events/942763/smart_tv_workshop_-_serge_egelman_research_slides.pdf. [Accessed 15 February 2017].

[29] Cyber Security, "How to easily hack your Smart TV: Samsung and LG," 7 July 2015. [Online]. Available: https://iicybersecurity.wordpress.com/2015/07/07/how-to-easily-hack-your-smart-tv-samsung-and-lg/.

Journal of The Colloquium for Information System Security Education (CISSE)
Edition 5, Issue 1 – October 2017

Teaching Cyber Resilience for Critical Infrastructure Systems

William Arthur Conklin[1]
waconklin@uh.edu

Anne Kohnke[2]
akohnke@ltu.edu

[1]College of Technology
University of Houston
Houston, TX

[2]College of Management
Lawrence Technological University
Southfield, MI

Abstract - Successful cyberattacks will occur no matter how much money and resources are dedicated to the problem. At the same time, the sectors in the current national infrastructure have not developed an effective standard strategy to protect themselves. The paradigm we present here argues that a cyberresilient strategy is an effective and cost-efficient approach to protecting the critical systems that power our way of life. This paper presents both a staged approach to implementing cyber-resilient systems as well as a general curriculum and pedagogy for disseminating this knowledge.

Keywords

Cybersecurity, Cyberresilient Strategy

1   INTRODUCTION

Cyberspace is full of adversaries ranging from state-sponsored hackers to skilled cybercriminals, to any person with a grudge and a connection to the Internet. Because of the proliferation of such threats, cyberattacks on the numerous elements of the U.S. critical infrastructure are a daily fact of life. For instance, the Industrial Control Systems-Computer Emergency Response Team (ICS-CERT) reports that U.S. industrial control systems were attacked at least 245 times over a 12-month period (OAS, 2015). In other parts of the world, a 2015 attack on Ukraine's power grid left 700,000 people without electricity (Brasso, 2016). The perpetrators of the Ukrainian attack were observed conducting similar attacks against the U.S. energy sector (Brasso, 2016). Although there was not an actual service disruption, many experts believe that those exploits were a probe for future moves on the U.S. infrastructure (Brasso, 2016).

The reason why the protection of our national infrastructure is so critically important is that a major exploit, like a successful cyberattack on the electrical grid, could leave the U.S. cloaked in darkness and unable to communicate without any form of twenty-first century transport. It would likely kill many thousands of citizens, perhaps millions, either through civil unrest, failure of public systems, or mass starvation (Brasso, 2016; Maynor, 2006).

Notwithstanding the disastrous nature of cyberattacks, the industries in our current national infrastructure have not developed coherent plans or effective strategies to protect themselves (Brasso, 2016). This includes the Chemical Sector; Commercial Facilities: Communications; Dams; the Defense Industrial Base; Emergency Services; Energy: Financial Services; Food and Agriculture; Government Facilities; Healthcare and Public Health; Information Technology; Nuclear Reactors, Materials, and Waste; Transportation; and Water and Wastewater Systems (PPD-21, 2013, p.2).

At the heart of the problem are the automated supervisory control and data acquisition (SCADA) systems that perform the myriad functions that underwrite our daily life. In the generic SCADA architecture, data from sensors or manual inputs are sent to programmable logic controllers (PLCs) or remote terminal units (RTUs), which then pass that information through to human operators along a SCADA network. The complex control networks are central to the day-to-day achievement of the purposes of each of these sectors and SCADA operations permit unified control of dispersed devices through standard protocols. SCADA is ubiquitous in the infrastructure in that these types of systems underwrite the remote operation of a wide variety of systems and services.

The rise of microprocessors and programmable logic controllers (PLCs) in the early 1970s allowed organizations to remotely control their automated processes. In the 1990s, the introduction of more sophisticated networking and PC-based interfaces resulted in local area network (LAN) based SCADA systems (Russel, 2017). This continuing dispersal inevitably morphed into wide area network (WAN) connections and the internet. This final step ensured real-time access to the operations of everything from, manufacturing assembly lines, to home heating systems, often through remote devices (IEEE, 2012). This type of access helps organizations and even individuals make data-driven decisions about their individual operations (Boyer, 2010).

SCADA utilizes multiple software processes and hardware elements to monitor operational behavior, gather data, and record the second-by-second actions of every machine and device in a SCADA supervised system (Van Hoa, 2016). Thus, the components of a SCADA system are diverse. In practice, SCADA systems can manage large-scale organizational operations over great distances at multiple sites. The diversity and the wide dispersal of the sensors and controllers that comprise a typical system make SCADA tempting targets for attack.

This is especially true because the PLCs and RTUs in a SCADA system are deployed without any consideration of their resistance to attack. Therefore, there have been long-standing concerns about the overall SCADA powered infrastructure being vulnerable to cyberwarfare and cyberterrorism attacks and is one reason why the cyber-resilience approach has gotten a lot of recent interest (Eisenhauer, 2006; Nat-Geo, 2017; Symantec, 2014; E-Y, 2014).

The cyber resilience approach is particularly suited to ensuring the continuing survivability of SCADA systems because the focus of a cyber resilient strategy is to maintain core functionality at all costs without consideration of defending less critical, or peripheral elements. The strict emphasis on survivability is the reason why cyber resilience, versus cybersecurity, is the approach of choice for critical systems.

Cybersecurity is based around ensuring all logical points of access to secure space whether electronic, human, or physical and normally requires an extensive resource commitment. Whereas, cyber resilience only ensures those elements that are deemed critical to system survival, this is particularly relevant to SCADA given the encapsulated, specific purpose function of most of the components in something like an electrical power system. In effect, each component's limited, well-defined purpose makes it easier to identify and protect only the critical elements.

Since the requirement to maintain the functioning of a few critical components is less resource intensive than the need to ensure the confidentiality, integrity and availability of all assets within secure space, cyber resilience is much more resource efficient. The narrowing of scope allows protection measures to be concentrated onto a far smaller attack surface, which theoretically ensures more effective protection for the things that simply can't be allowed to fail.

2   THE SEVEN STAGES OF CYBER RESILIENCY

Cyber resilience is founded on classification, prioritization, and comprehensive strategic policy-based deployment of a rigorous set of real-world security controls (Symantec, 2014). Cyber resilience involves the creation of a set of well-defined processes, which react to penetrations of the organizational perimeter (US-CERT, 2016). These standard processes are both electronic and behavioral in focus and they are designed to protect key assets, as well as ensure optimum recovery of the overall system in the event of successful attack (Symantec, 2014). This process is embodied in seven generic principles shown in Figure 1 (Conklin, Shoemaker, & Kohnke, 2017).

Figure 1, The Seven Stages of Cyber Resiliency

1. *Classify*—If assets are not identified, they cannot be protected therefore, all SCADA system assets must be identified, labeled, and arrayed in a coherent baseline of "things." This baseline describes all potential protection targets and it is maintained under strict configuration management. This is comparable to the "Classification" phase of the NIST Risk Management Framework (NISTb, 2014) and embodies the dictates of FIPS 199 (NISTa, 2004).

2. *Risk*—Resiliency requires appropriate situational awareness. Therefore, a broad-spectrum risk assessment must be performed that characterizes all known threat scenarios as they apply to the identified asset base of the SCADA system. This is a risk assessment process comparable to the "Security Assessment" phase of NIST SP 800-53a (NIST SP 800-53A Rev.4, 2014).

3. *Rank*—Assets in which the SCADA system absolutely can not afford to have compromised are selected, evaluated and a provably effective countermeasure response is deployed for each of the chosen assets. This is primarily an engineering design exercise, driven by knowledge of the components and their inter-relationships which was obtained in the "Classify" phase. Resources are focused on assuring only those components that are designated as critical. The resources that are left over are then allocated to protection and recovery of the rest of the system. This is analogous to the "Select" phase of the NIST Risk Management Framework (NISTb, 2014).

4. *Deploy*—The functionality to ensure resilience must be baked-into the architecture of the SCADA system in such a way that critical functions are assured; presuming a largely successful attack. This is a pure design/control deployment exercise comparable to the "Implement" phase of the NIST Risk Management Framework (NISTb, 2014) but control design and deployment are based on the recommendations for

the relevant baselines as specified in NIST 800-53(4), (NIST SP 800-53A Rev.4, 2014).

5. *Test*—the SCADA system's architectural resilience must be assured. This is a planning and oversight function that characterizes the effectiveness of critical control performance against stated mission goals. Methods like penetration testing apply here. This is an assessment process comparable to the "Assess" phase of the NIST Risk Management Framework (NISTb, 2014).

6. *Recover*—Well-defined processes are documented and established to ensure that all of the SCADA systems functions are fully restored within requisite parameters. This is comparable to the "Plan-Purpose-Scope-Relationship" recommendations embodied in NIST SP 800-37 Rev. 1 (NISTc, 2010) and it embodies metrics suitable to evaluate disaster recovery performance (Bradford, 2017).

7. *Evolve*—The organization dynamically adjusts the SCADA system's cyber-resilient architecture based on lessons learned. This is comparable to the implementation of the NIST Cyber Security Framework process (NIST-CSF, 2014).

3   EMBEDDING CYBER RESILIENCE INTO HOW WE EDUCATE

Even though this commonly accepted seven-stage model specifies a viable evolutionary process for developing cyber-resilience in SCADA systems, it still lacks practical application. Therefore, to ensure that cyber-resilience is put into practice, the details about the specific activities and tasks that need to be performed must be widely disseminated in a complete and coherent fashion, which has been the traditional role of professional education and training.

The knowledge, skill, and ability (KSA) requirements for each of the requisite functions in this staged model must be fleshed out to educate practitioners about the steps necessary to create a cyber-resilient process. We have chosen to present the structuring and delivery of a model curriculum for cyber-resilience organized by the seven generic stages of the process.

3.1 Principle 1: Classify

In some respects, cyber resilience is nothing more than a specialized continuity management solution. The aim of cyber-resilience is to maintain critical organizational functions at all costs. In this respect, the decisions that come out of the cyber resilience classification process will determine how the business will invest its precious time and resources. Thus, the identification process is perhaps the most important step in creating a cyber-resilient organization because the outcome of the classification process will drive every subsequent protection action.

The key to cyber resilience is understanding what constitutes core functionality in each system and that is essentially an engineering design issue. All computerized systems are complex and highly interdependent so the essence of success lies in the identification of just those essential functions and relationships necessary to ensure basic system survival. Accordingly, a deliberate and formally documented classification activity is the logical starting point. Cyber resilience assumes that all systems will eventually be compromised. Given this assumption, the cyber resilience function ensures specifically targeted controls. These controls are designed to ensure that only the critical subset of functions essential to the continuing operation of the system are fully protected, even if all other system activities are compromised. This is an organization-wide exercise whose aim is to understand the criticality, sensitivity, and priority of all items in the asset base. It involves all stakeholders because buy-in is an essential condition for embedding changes in the organization.

Along with the mandate to ensure the survival of core functionality, the cyber resilience identification process also defines straightforward and effective paths to restore any of the lower priority functions that might have been lost in the actual compromise. For instance, the PLC is the key element in a sensor array. If it is lost, then all the sensors are lost. Consequently, its survival is critical, whereas loss of a given sensor might be acceptable if it does not monitor some other function that is deemed critical. The identification and dependency process is the logic that a student must understand to perform a capable triage of system components. The specific practices for doing that are explicitly outlined in the classification process that is described in FIPS 199 (NISTa, 2004).

3.2 Principle 2: Risk

Risk assessment provides timely and accurate understanding of the threat status of all critical system components. This is essentially a risk assessment function. Risk assessments identify and evaluate all potential threats on a given attack surface. The evaluation then drives the engineering decisions about the best way to ensure the requisite continuity. The aim is to fully understand every conceivable threat, incident, natural or manmade events, that warrants a targeted protection mechanism. This includes natural disasters, cyber incidents, acts of terrorism, sabotage, and destructive criminal activity targeting critical components of the enterprise infrastructure (PDD-21, 2014). The outcome of this phase is a detailed map of the threat environment, sufficient to support good engineering decisions with respect to explicit protection approaches.

For instructors who require a structured model of the process, the security control assessment approach outlined in NIST 800-53(4) is an excellent template for understanding the steps involved in structuring and conducting a robust and comprehensive risk assessment process (NIST SP 800-53A Rev.4, 2014). The recommendations are detailed as well as logical and can be easily transferred into a unit on risk assessment for digital threat identification and evaluation. The added advantage of adopting 800-53 as the model is that its recommendations fit very well with all of the other relevant NIST standards in this area.

3.3 Principle 3: Rank

Prioritization is the next logical step in the cyber-resilience process. Once the organization's assets have been identified and baselined and the threat environment characterized, the criticality of all assets in the system is ranked. For SCADA, this is a targeted ranking process that focuses only on that specific system. This is also an engineering design activity however, it should involve all stakeholders because all engineering activity takes place in a business environment that might be more political than logical.

SCADA functioning might impact any associated person, process, technology, or facility that is involved in the business however, some system assets are more critical to simple survival than others. Therefore, the ranking process must authoritatively identify, document, and ensure only those components whose loss would compromise the system's mission, vision, values and purposes (PDD-21, 2014). Unfortunately, ranking can turn into a political free-for-all where various stakeholders attempt to enforce their own agendas. Obviously, this cannot be allowed to happen if the eventual architectural solution is going to be truly resilient. Therefore, criticality must be understood based on a clear map of system functions and dependencies, which are referenced in an objective and rational way to the mission and goals of the organization.

From a teaching standpoint, a rigorous set of protection requirements are specified for just those assets that directly enable the organizational mission. Rigor is defined as the ability to resist any known or conceivable method of attack (PDD-21, 2014). Protection mechanisms are specified and designed to maintain the uninterrupted functioning of each system asset within the cyber resilience protection scheme. A detailed discussion outlining the requisite KSAs for the selection process is provided in the "Select" section of NIST SP-800-37(1) (NISTc, 2010, p.24).

3.4 Principle 4: Deploy

The deploy stage focuses on the specific controls required to make a critical asset resilient. At the generic level, this is a strategic governance process. Deploy creates and then embeds the substantive controls that have been developed to effectively ensure the mission, goals and objectives of a given infrastructure system. In this phase, the explicit control set for each critical asset is substantively created and deployed.

Additionally, this stage prioritizes those objectives and implements targeted control actions to most effectively achieve priority objectives. It then analyzes and assesses the deployed control set to ensure that the resultant infrastructure satisfies the critical purpose. If documented control objectives are not met, then the Deployment process undertakes the necessary analysis to modify controls, or plug gaps. A detailed discussion outlining the requisite KSAs for the deployment process is provided in the "Implement" section of NIST SP-800-37(1) (NISTc, 2010, p.28).

3.5 Principle 6: Recover

This stage focuses on continuity management. The goal of recovery planning is to ease the impact of disruptive events for all aspects of the system and is accomplished by developing and executing a well-established set of plans to ensure rapid restoration of non-critical services (PDD-21, 2014). To achieve this end, the overall system operating environment is studied to identify all potential failure modes and then a proper strategy is developed to recover from potential breakdowns, or disruptions.

The goal is to create a complete and effective recovery process that will address all plausible types of compromises to the non-critical elements of the system. The plan for incident recovery must be explicit for each asset and lessons learned are compiled to develop improvement strategies. This requires an operational plan capable of identifying, analyzing, responding to, escalating and learning from all adverse incidents. A detailed discussion outlining the requisite

KSAs for the deployment process is provided in NIST SP-800-34(1) (NISTd, 2010).

3.6 Principle 7: Evolve

The Evolve stage serves as the formal basis for identifying and deploying process and technological responses and improvements across the organization. Evolution is required to continue to maintain the organization's cyber resilience goals as the threat picture changes. In this stage, measurable improvements that could increase the resilience of critical assets are identified, analyzed, and systematically deployed. The effects of currently deployed processes and technology improvements are measured and the effectiveness of the selected process improvement is characterized. The five functions that must be executed mirror those of the NIST Cyber Security Framework (NIST-CSF, 2014).

Evolution is driven by the collection and analysis of data from lessons learned about the day-to-day execution of the resilience process. Improvement recommendations are supported by data obtained from the deployment of prior process and technology controls. Nevertheless, because this is essentially a "maintenance," activity this type of analysis involves ongoing testing and risk estimation. Lessons-learned typically involve objectively evaluating the performance of deployed processes against plans, objectives, standards, and procedures; as well as the outcomes of organizational innovation and deployment process. US-CERT provides a template for itemizing the steps of an organizational review and evolution process. The steps and requisite capabilities are outlined in detail and provide excellent material for a systematic evolution process (US-CERT, 2016).

4 CONCLUSION

The increased presence of advanced cyber threats makes it inevitable that all organizations will ultimately be targeted (OAS, 2015). Cyber resilience recognizes that there are too many advanced hacking tools to prevent sophisticated attackers from finding the cracks in even the most robust cyber-security system (Lois, 2015). The concept of cyber-resilience goes far beyond the classic boundaries of better hardware and software access controls (EY, 2014). Instead, organizations establish a "cyber resilience strategy" that gives them the ability to withstand and recover rapidly from disruptive events (EY, 2014).

Practically speaking, the best argument for cyber-resilience is that it concentrates resources where they will make the most difference. This is particularly germane to SCADA in that any attack on an infrastructure element threatens a lot more than simple business processes. Thus, cyber-resilience is a particularly important aspect of ensuring survival and easing recovery of the critical systems that underwrite our way-of-life. Accordingly, cyber resilience requires the organization to spend whatever it takes to develop a well-defined, explicit set of controls to ensure survival of only those critical elements that cannot be compromised. The controls must assure provable protection of core functionality and the various interdependencies in the enterprise's eco-system (EY, 2014).

It is our belief that little substantive education has taken place when it comes to protecting the critical infrastructure, particularly as it applies to SCADA systems. There is no standard model for good educational practice that provide guidelines or best practices of how to reliably protect critical infrastructure components, given the inevitability of failure in traditional approaches. The ideas presented here are a start toward eventually overcoming this lack of knowledge. It presents a process and a framework for structuring and communicating standard cyber-resilience best practice to the educational community at large.

REFERENCES

[1] Bradford, C. (2017), *Disaster Recovery Metrics: What They Are and How to Use Them*, Recovery Zone, [online] http://www.storagecraft.com/blog/disaster-recovery-metrics-use/ .

[2] Boyer, S. A. (2010). In *SCADA Supervisory Control and Data Acquisition. USA: ISA - International Society of Automation.* ISBN 978-1-936007-09-7.

[3] Brasso, B. (2016). *Cyber Attacks Against Critical Infrastructure Are No Longer Just Theories*, [online], Fire-Eye, [online] https://www.fireeye.com/blog/executive-perspective/2016/04/cyber_attacks_agains.html .

[4] Conklin, W.A., Shoemaker, D. and Kohnke, A. (2017), *Cyber Resilience: Rethinking Cybersecurity Strategy to Build a Cyber Resilient Architecture*, Paper presentation at the 12th International Conference on Cyber Warfare and Security, Dayton, OH

[5] Eisenhauer, J., Donnelly, P., Ellis, M., and O'Brien, M (2006). *Roadmap to Secure Control Systems in the Energy Sector*, Energetics Incorporated, Sponsored by the U.S. Department of Energy and the U.S. Department of Homeland Security.

[6] EY. (2014). *Achieving Resilience in the Cyber Ecosystem*, [online], Ernst and Young, [online] http://www.ey.com/Publication/vwLUAssets/cyber_ecosystem/$FILE/EY-Insights_on_GRC_Cyber_ecosystem.pdf .

[7] IEEE. (2012). *Introduction to Industrial Control Networks*. IEEE Communications Surveys and Tutorials, [online] PDF.

[8] Lois, J. E. (2015). *It Can Happen to You: Know the Anatomy of a Cyber Intrusion.* Navy Cyber Defense Operations Command (NCDOC), Story Number: NNS151019-05, Release Date: 10/19/2015.

[9] Maynor and R. Graham (2006). *SCADA Security and Terrorism: We're Not Crying Wolf*, X-Force, Black Hat, [online] /BH-Fed-06-Maynor-Graham-up-1.pdf

[10] Nat-Geo. (2017). *American Blackout*. National Geographic Channel, [online] http://channel.nationalgeographic.com/american-blackout/

[11] NISTa (2004). FIPS 199 *Federal Information Processing Standard Publication 199, Standards for Security Categorization of Federal Information and Information Systems.* Gaithersburg, MD: National Institute of Standards and Technology.

[12] NISTb (2014). *Risk Management Framework*. Gaithersburg, MD: National Institute of Standards and Technology.

[13] NISTc. (2010). *NIST Special Publication 800-37 Revision 1, Guide for Applying the Risk Management Framework to Federal Information Systems, A Security Life Cycle Approach*. Gaithersburg, MD: National Institute of Standards and Technology

[14] NIST-CSF. (2014), *Cyber Security Framework*, Gaithersburg, MD: National Institute of Standards and Technology.

[15] NISTd. (2010), *NIST Special Publication 800-34 Rev. 1, Contingency Planning Guide for Federal Information Systems*. Gaithersburg, MD: National Institute of Standards and Technology.

[16] NIST SP 800-53A Rev.4. (2014) *Assessing Security and Privacy Controls in Federal Information Systems and Organizations Building Effective Assessment Plans*, Gaithersburg, MD: National Institute of Standards and Technology.

[17] OAS. (2015). *Report on Cybersecurity and Critical Infrastructure in the Americas, Organization of American States*, Trend Micro Incorporated, [online] https://www.trendmicro.com/cloud-content/us/pdfs/security-intelligence/reports/critical-infrastructures-west-hemisphere.pdf .

[18] PPD-21. (2013). *Presidential Policy Directive 21: Critical Infrastructure Security and Resilience* [online], The White House, [online] https://www.whitehouse.gov/the-press-office/2013/02/12/presidential-policy-directive-critical-infrastructure-security-and-resil .

[19] Russel, J. (2015). *A Brief History of SCADA/EMS*. [online] http://scadahistory.com/.

[20] Symantec. (2014) *A Manifesto for Cyber Resilience*, Symantec, [online] https://www.symantec.com/content/en/us/enterprise/other_resources/b-a-manifesto-for-cyber-resilience.pdf .

[21] US-CERT. (2016) *Cyber Resilience Review (CRR)*, Department of Homeland Security, [online] https://www.us-cert.gov/sites/default/files/c3vp/crr-fact-sheet.pdf .

[22] Van Hoa, N., Tran, Q. T., and Besanger, Y. (2016), *SCADA as a service approach for interoperability of micro-grid platforms*. Sustainable Energy, Grids and Network. doi: 10.1016/j.segan.2016.08.001.

Journal of The Colloquium for Information System Security Education (CISSE)
Edition 5, Issue 1 - October 2017

The Calculus of Cyber Warfare as Influenced by the Subtle Art of Military Theory

David R. Shaw
dshaw@cyberba.net

Jeff Carr
jeff@suitsandspooks.com

Tom Muehleisen
tmuehleisen@cyberba.net

University of Washington
Center for Information Assurance and Cybersecurity
Bothell, WA

Abstract - Ever since The "History of the Peloponnesian War as written by Thucydides, an Athenian historian who also happened to serve as an Athenian general during the war, we have intellectually feasted upon progressive war theories throughout the ages. Conventional war is generally considered a three-dimensional endeavor. With the advent of cyber warfare, we add a fourth dimension of silent, asymmetric proportions, normally conducted by nation-states waged against one another. This war is currently being fought on a global scale endangering the security of many States and organizations. We face a vicious cyber offense with no rules of engagement and defend with a cyber defense system that labors valiantly under layers of rules, regulations, and oversight that is legacy from decades back, slow to progress to match the speed and efficiency of the cyber threat.

The authors of this paper seek to address the cyber threat from a military perspective, adapting time proven strategic military theory and theorists concepts of conventional warfare to principles of cyber warfare.

General Terms

Military Theory, Cybersecurity

Keywords

Military, Cyber, Cybersecurity, Cyberwar

1 INTRODUCTION

Recent headlines such as *"The New Handbook for Cyberwar is Being Written by Russia"* [1], *"How China is preparing for cyberwar"* [2], and *"Cyber nationalism and the new world order"* [3] puts a bright light on the global shift from threats of a conventional war somewhere remote to the "civilized" nations to a hyper threat of a technology war targeted directly at our Nation State, and has elevated to the probability of ONE affecting all in its path. The governments in North America and Europe have been working furiously to armor their high value systems with a focus on cybersecurity that is totally unprecedented.

By applying military theories and styles to cybersecurity and risk management frameworks for government agencies, we are making it infinitely more difficult for the threat actors to achieve success in their attacks. However, the private sector remains almost completely vulnerable to loss during a cyber war or similar level of attack which will literally cripple our national economy when hit with a massive attack. The global financial depression of 2008 provides us with an insight to this claim as to consequences.

The cyber risk management emphasis in the private sector has been largely through the Information Sharing and Analysis Centers (ISACS) coalescing the larger members of the commercial businesses. Certain sectors of the nation's private sector, including the public utilities, and other NGO's, are levered into compliance of antiquated regulations and processes by audit and regulatory oversight. Likewise, most commercial businesses who have structured risk management and incident response plans are not testing them regularly and therefore leave the data protection and response from incursions to their technology managers, or ignore the risk.

The problem is mammoth and the ability to thwart the threat against the private sector critical infrastructure is well beyond the scope of any government or similar sized entity to solve externally. Therefore, the problem must be solved from within the confines of the individual businesses with totally unconventional means.

We are therefore advocating adapting principles of military style attributes and well established military theories to businesses that will harmonize their protection of critical data and resources, maintain cybersecurity pace with the threat actors and threat vectors enveloping virtually every sector of our technology. This adaptation may also armor against devastating losses that are causing over 60% of the business attacked to fail within 6 month of the attack.

This paper advances that the calculus of cyber warfare can be likened to the theoretical military style frameworks devised, tested and embedded in conventional warfare. President George W. Bush stated: "Cyberspace is the nervous system—the control system of our country" [4], Cyber aggression upon our national interests, including our manufacturing and service industries, and critical infrastructures can and should be considered as an act of war. Thus, we have adopted principles and theories of warfare to the framework of cyber warfare, which is in its adolescent stage of growth and dynamics.

2 APPLICABLE MILITARY THEORIES

2.1 Past and Present: Clausewitz and Luttwak

Carl Philipp Gottfried (or Gottlieb) von Clausewitz was a Prussian general and military theorist who stressed the "moral" (meaning, in modern terms, psychological) and political aspects of war. His most notable work, Vom Kriege (*On War*), was unfinished at his death. Clausewitz was a realist in many different senses and, while in some respects a romantic, also drew heavily on the rationalist ideas of the European Enlightenment. He stressed the dialectical interaction of diverse factors, noting how unexpected developments unfolding under the "fog of war" (i.e., in the face of incomplete, dubious, and often completely erroneous information and high levels of fear, doubt, and excitement) call for rapid decisions by alert commanders [5].

Drawing from the theoretical treatments in his book *On War*, one is challenged from the onset of Book 1 to draw multiple direct parallels to cyber warfare from his theories, assertions and aphorisms. However, Clausewitz has provided us with some grist for our comparative mill. My favorite is the following equation (Figure 1) that is paraphrased or adapted as The Calculus of Cyber Warfare, phrased as:

Figure 1: The Total Power to Wage Cyber War (of two opponents)

As directed to cyber warfare, the "means" relates directly to the skills, tools, access, funding, and all that the threat actor can possibly bring against a target or targets which is described by Clausewitz as the maximum exertion of strength. The "will" factors in the intangibles or non-material force multipliers such as mobilizing moral forces which often are fungible with national politics for nation-state threat actors. An additional factor are the rules of engagement which are often obviated by the threat actor(s) which gives them an additional advantage over a constrained cyber defense system / process.

The defender must employ at least equal resources and amass will throughout the organization to fend off any and all attacks by the threat actors, regardless of their skill levels. The objective is for the targeted business (face it, we are all targeted), to identify its key high value assets and build a defense in depth to make it infinitely difficult for threat actors to penetrate. Lastly, there needs to be an enterprise wide understanding of the threats and defense postures to Harmonize the risk management leadership / command structure from top to bottom with a firm understanding of their respective roles, responsibilities and relationships (3 R's) regarding cybersecurity. This goes to both Means and Will to "get it right" every time.

The following image (Figure 2) is a sample of cybersecurity defense in depth demonstrating means and a certain degree of will by virtue of the type of defense.

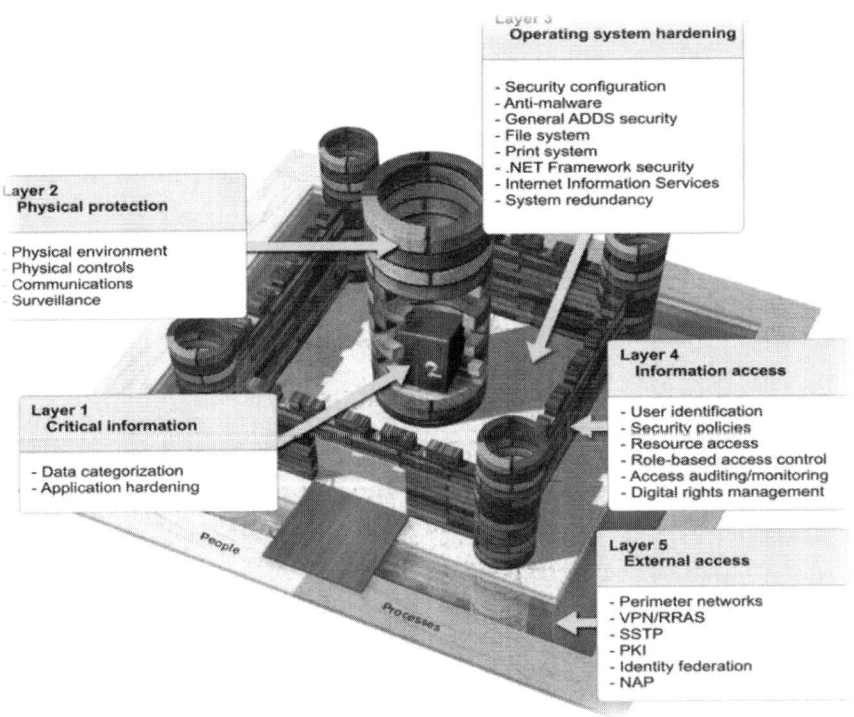

Figure 2: Castle Defense System – Defense in Depth [6]

The "C-Suite" must identify the high value units (HVUs) in the entity to be protected. Then Clausewitz's theory of Means x Will is invoked as outlined above to protect the HVUs) as the Iron Calculus of Cyber Warfare.

Edward Luttwak is both a celebrated author ("Coup D'Etat: A Practical Handbook", "Strategy: The Logic of War and Peace") and a consultant to modern-day governments on the application of strategy in warfare [7]. This article references his book "Strategy: The Logic of War and Peace" from the perspective of defending against attacks in cyberspace where the principals of "least expectation" and "deception" certainly apply.

"Least expectation", according to Luttwak, is the practice of understanding what an adversary expects you to do, and then doing the opposite. This is contradictory to the logic of peacetime when, if you wish to travel from point A to point B, you take the most direct route, using the best roads at a time of day that has the least amount of traffic. However, when you have an adversary whose mission is to intercept and engage you, you'll want to travel on the worst roads, in the middle of the night with no moon, and in heavy rain. Luttwak's entire first chapter is dedicated to this contrary logic where "a bad road can be considered good precisely because it is bad" [8].

One of the emerging strategies in network defense is the use of deception, which has come a long way from the use of honey pots. Gartner predicts that by 2018, 10 percent of enterprises will be using a form of this technology from one of a handful of cybersecurity startups focused on delivering new deception tools and techniques [9].

Deception as a network defense strategy presumes that the defender can fool the attacker in believing that a server or the nodes on a server are an authentic part of the network and contain valuable data of interest to the attacker when in fact the server traps the attacker in a contained zone on the network where his actions can be studied safely for as long as the illusion can be sustained.

Unfortunately, there are two big obstacles to a successful deception defense. One is that you need to know what the attacker is interested in so that you can create an enticing trap. The other is that you need to dedicate resources to creating a compelling illusion that will be believable to an experienced attacker. Those resources pull from the overall Security Operations Centre (SOC) budget, usually limited to begin with.

"More commonly, the use of (passive) dummies and (active) decoys of any kind, from fake tanks and guns or complete unites, to flying or navigating decoys that simulate specific aircraft or submarines, are much cheaper than the real thing but still absorb resources that would otherwise increase the strength on hand." [10]

A third consideration in evaluating deception as a strategy, according to Luttwak, is that "deception deceives when there is a predisposition to deception" [11]. In network warfare, deception is the adversary's bread and butter. The use of a spear phishing attack to fool the intended victim into opening a poisoned document or visiting a website that serves malware is the most common way that organizations find themselves breached.

When a SOC is fighting an adversary who understands the tactics of deception so thoroughly, its own deception strategy will require substantial thought and planning in order for it to work. Even if it is successful in stopping the first attack, it will need to be revised in order to stop the second, and so on.

The hard truth is that, in time, a dedicated adversary with sufficient resources will gain access to the victim's network. For that reason, the best approach is not to waste resources on keeping adversaries out, but instead focus those resources on keeping the organization's crown jewels from leaving.

2.2 The OODA Loop

Decision process is a critical feature in defending against cyber-attacks. The OODA loop was developed by a fighter pilot tactician and is a formalized decision making procedure that is applied to any situation where a practiced decision-making process is necessary in a threat situation. It is especially important when the decisions have to be made quickly, as in a threat situation. The development of a rapid, agile decision making process is essential for cyber threats and can provide huge tactical advantages. Most entities when confronted with cyber threats / attacks take a "chess player role" where they make a move and wait for the threat actor to make a counter-move. To establish an effective defense posture against cyber threats, decisive moves should be as rapid as possible to keep the threat off balance and keep the initiative on side of the defender.

O-O-D-A stands for Observe-Orient-Decide-Act. It is a "loop" because it is repeated until the situation is over or the objective is satisfied (in some instances, the process is continuous and may never be satisfied). The objective is to work through the loop faster than a threat actor to gain or maintain a tactical advantage. In an ideal situation, a threat should be dealt with before the threat actor has even realized he is in a confrontational situation and entered his own OODA loop; this is a defense-in-depth situation. If in a reactive posture and the threat actor has initiated the attack, the objective is to "get inside" his loop to gain an effective advantage followed by a continued exercise of the process to fortify the advantage.

This looping concept referred to the ability possessed by fighter pilots that allowed them to succeed in combat via a rapid and agile decision process. The OODA Loop is now used as a standard framework or methodology by military, federal and commercial entities as a basis for rapid and continuous assessment and decision making. The premise of the model is that decision-making is the result of rational behavior in which problems are viewed as a cycle of

Observation, Orientation (situational awareness), Decision Making, and Action. Boyd diagramed the OODA loop as shown in Figure 3 below:

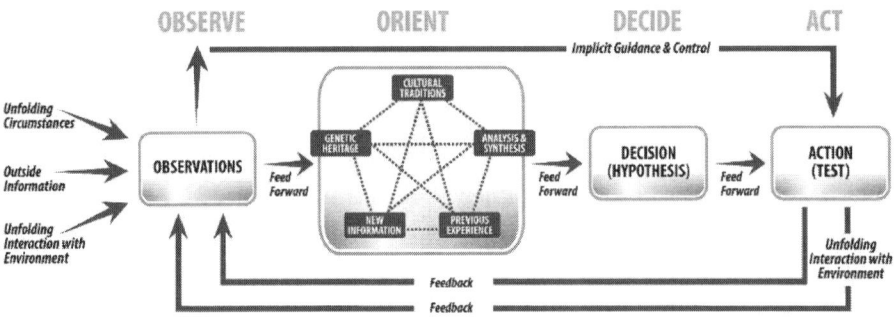

Figure 3: Standard OODA Loop Functional Diagram

An entity (whether an individual or an organization) that can process this cycle more quickly than an opponent can "get inside" the opponent's decision cycle and gain the advantage. The essential components of the OODA Loop as depicted in the above figure are:

- **Observation**: Scan the whole environment and gather information from it.

- **Orientation**: Use the information to form a mental image of the circumstances. That is, synthesize the data into information. As more information is received, one may "deconstruct" old images and then "create" new images. Note that different people require different levels of details to perceive an event. It is often implied that the reason people cannot make good decisions is that people are bad decisions makers — much akin to saying that the reason some people cannot drive is that they are bad drivers. However, most bad decisions result from the fact that a person will often fail to place the information that is available into its proper context. Orientation emphasizes the context in which events occur, so that it may facilitate decisions and actions.

174

That is, orientation helps to turn information into knowledge, and knowledge, not information, is the real predictor of making good decisions.

- **Decision**: Consider options and select a subsequent course of action or actions.

- **Action**: Carry out the conceived decision. Once the result of the action is observed, the entire cycle starts over. Note that in combat (or competing against the competition), you want to cycle through the four steps faster and better than the enemy, hence, it is a loop.

The Loop doesn't mean that individuals or organizations have to observe, orient, decide, and act, in the order as shown in the diagram above. Rather, picture the loop as an interactive feedback web with orientation at the core, as shown in the diagram below. Orientation is how a situation is interpreted, based on culture, experience, new information, analysis, synthesis, and heritage.

The Loop is a set of interacting loops that are kept in continuous operation thus the decision process is agile, capable of rapid assessment, and can encompass multiple perspectives as discussed below.

It has been generally stated that nation-states operation like biological organisms composed of discrete systems. These systems include leadership, organic essentials, infrastructure, population, and the military. A Hungarian immigrant, Brigadier General Huba Wass de Czege (pronounced VOSH de tsay-guh) (born August 13, 1941) is the son of Count Albert Wass de Szentegyed et Czege. Wass de Czege retired from the United States Army as a General Officer with a reputation as a highly innovative thinker. He is the founder and first director of the School of Advanced Military Studies at the United States Army Command and General Staff College [12]. He stated that Positive Ends is the possibility of taking advantage of a new security environment to create conditions for long-term peace.

175

The adaptation of this theory goes to enveloping a new strategic risk management framework, policy and process with advanced tools to create a longer-term threat avoidance and protect organizational HVUs and E-Systems. Cyber-attacks generally may appear to be chaotic and are asymmetric, requiring a highly dynamic tool(s) and processes to assess and visualize them. Whether successful or unsuccessful, such attacks can be devastating and have the capability to create havoc in what has become our fundamental infrastructure for communication and commerce. From simple email, to social networks, from e-business to critical intelligence gathering, nearly every aspect of modern operations rely on systems potentially exposed to cyber threats. Identifying potential vulnerabilities, performing risk analysis, and subsequently building cyber defense systems in depth are essential steps to protect high value E-Systems.

Key attributes for risk analysis methods and tools for cyber threat modeling include the following:

- **Agility**: The ability of the risk assessment process to accept and analyze dynamic threats from an asymmetric attack environment. Attack surfaces or threat vectors are not always clearly defined therefore agility is a necessary feature in any cyber risk assessment process. This includes discovery of new attack surfaces via an iterative testing process which addresses the issue of "we don't know what we don't know".

- **Proactivity**: The ability to take the initiative by acting rather than reacting to threat actors and cyber-attacks. Take offensive action to either preoccupy the opposition and ultimately its ability to directly harm or destroy its ability to attack.

- **Resiliency & Elasticity**: The ability to recover quickly and accurately from setbacks and changes.

- **Rapid assessment capability**: Rapidly changing technologies and their applications (including methods of application) demand a capability to rapidly assess attack surfaces and associated threat vectors.

- **Scalable**: The capability of a system to increase total throughput under an increased load when resources are added. It also needs to address the scope of the analysis to include subsystems, system and/or system of systems.

- **Center of Gravity**: The hub of all power and movement on which everything depends, the point at which all energies should be directed. Focus is a key attribute in protecting HVUs and combating cyber-attacks.

2.3 Sun Tzu and Cyber War

No essay addressing military theory can go without engaging Sun Tzu. His *The Art of War* is an ancient Chinese military treatise dating from the 5th century BC. Attributed to the ancient Chinese military strategist Sun Tzu. It is commonly thought of as a definitive work on military strategy and tactics…and has long been the most influential strategy text in East Asia. It has had an influence on Eastern and Western military thinking, business tactics, legal strategy and beyond for centuries [13]. Selected Sun Tzu quotes from *The Art of War* applicable to cyber warfare are presented as follows and having digested the above theoretical attributes generate a kinship to those concepts and associated principles as are noted in italics:

- "Appear weak when you are strong, and strong when you are weak." *(Relates to Clausewitz)*

- "If you know the enemy *(threat and threat actor)* and know yourself, you need not fear the result of a hundred battles. If you know yourself but not the enemy, for every *(cyber)* victory gained you will also suffer a defeat. If you know neither the enemy nor yourself, you will succumb in every battle *(cyber-attack)*."

- "Supreme excellence consists of breaking the enemy's resistance without fighting."

- "If your enemy is secure at all points, be prepared for him. If he is in superior strength, evade him. If your opponent is temperamental, seek to irritate him. Pretend to be weak, that he may grow arrogant. If he is taking his ease, give him no rest. If his forces are united, separate them. If sovereign and subject are in accord, put division between them. Attack him where he is unprepared, appear where you are not expected."

- "Engage people *(threat actor)* with what they expect; it is what they are able to discern and confirms their projections. It settles them into predictable patterns of response, occupying their minds while you wait for the extraordinary moment — that which they cannot anticipate."

- "The art of *(cyber)* war is of vital importance to the State. It is a matter of life and death, a road either to safety or to ruin. Hence it is a subject of inquiry which can on no account be neglected."

2.4 Military Information Operations

We conclude the section with the present by defining something DoD calls the Information Environment (IE). "The information environment is the aggregate of individuals, organizations, and systems that collect, process, disseminate, or act on information. This environment consists of three interrelated dimensions, which continuously interact with individuals, organizations, and systems. These dimensions are known as physical, informational, and cognitive. The physical dimension is composed of command and control systems, key decision makers, and supporting infrastructure that enable individuals and organizations to create effects. The informational dimension specifies where and how information is collected, processed, stored, disseminated, and protected. The cognitive dimension encompasses the minds of those who transmit, receive, and respond to or act on information." [15]

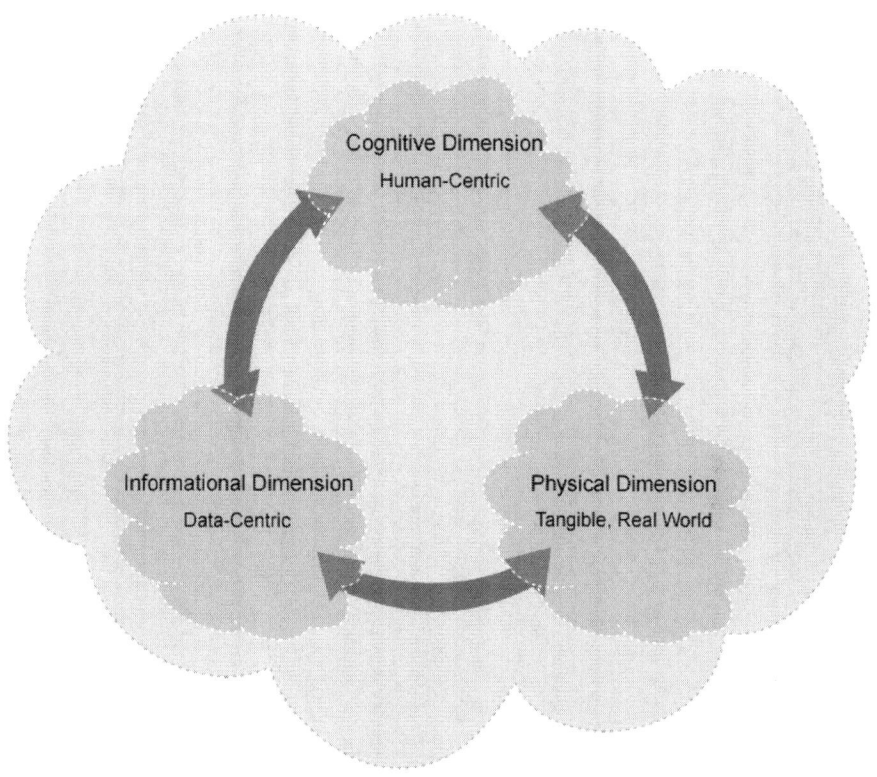

Figure 4: The Information Environment [16]

Spend a few moments considering the figure above and re-read the DoD definition. Each of these dimensions are important, and what is sometimes lost in this discussion of the "cyber" domain is that, ultimately, this information is used by a person. For a reason. The author's contention is that organizations will be more successful if they strictly control the who's and the why's, along with the what's and the where's. (translation: use proven methods like OPSEC [17] to identify what is important, who else wants it, what they can get to and what you can do to protect it). Further, that current DoD doctrine, the culmination of centuries of study and practice is extremely useful and applicable to civilian organizations.

3   DERIVED PRINCIPLES FROM MILITARY THEORY AS MAY BE ADAPTED TO CYBERSECURITY

Following an analysis of selected military theories proffered above, we offer key principles of cybersecurity for defense of our high value units (HVUs) within business and/or government entities to help defend against all levels cyber threat:

- Harmonize the risk management leadership / command structure from top to bottom with a firm understanding of their respective roles, responsibilities and relationships (3 R's). This is essential to ensure unified command and control, particularly in the time of crisis. No military goes without this clearly understood with each level having a complete understanding of the mission, their role(s) and the reporting structure.

- Adapt the best risk management model and framework for the business. This goes to mission, what is being protected, and the plans that support the mission.

- Devise and adopt rules of engagement (ROE) for combating cyber threat particular to the entity targeted. The ROE must be clearly understood by everyone in the chain of command.

- Exercise the incident response plan and with all stakeholders often with red and blue team participation at all levels. This goes to training, vulnerability assessment and recovery.

- Continually address tool assessment and realignment. This goes to agile protection, cost abatement, training, and effectivity of the adopted tools. Use Case Studies are an excellent means for tool assessment and getting all of the appropriate stakeholders to understand the results.

- Understand the continuous cyber related intelligence offered from deep technology data to business applications. This requires highly trained researchers and analysts to explore the cyber threat, apply the threat knowledge by mapping the threat against the organizational needs and vulnerabilities.

- Cybersecurity training and education, to include certifications, is continual. The cyber threat is dynamic therefore our understanding of the threat and how we adapt our defenses is a journey, not a destination.

- Consider the military theories proffered in this paper and if any or all resonate with your particular business environment and cyber threat posture we invite further study into the adoption of them into your business processes from a people, technology, process and strategic perspective.

- Just like the military, cybersecurity and risk management is a culture. And likewise, it is a journey of many dynamic attributes and never a destination.

- We are _all_ at cyber risk… therefore we need to ensure that processes to protect from cyber threat are understood and are dynamically cooperative in creating a resilient defense. In so doing we seize the initiative in creating innovative protections for all critical organizational infrastructures.

Figure 4: Cyber Warfare Takes on a Whole New Perspective [14]

4   FUTURE WORK

Cyber warfare is an emerging science from the business perspective in both government and the private sectors. The concepts introduced in this paper will be entertained as potential course content in certificate and advanced cybersecurity and risk management courses. Secondly, the authors will approach the Professional Military Schools to further expand these concepts by the Service Professionals attending these schools.

REFERENCES

[1] Sheera Frenkel, BussFeed News Reporter, BuzzFeed News, March 19, 2017

[2] Adam Segal, Contributor, The Christian Science Monitor, March 20, 2017

[3] John Costello, GCN Magazine, March 20, 2017

[4] George W. Bush, National Strategy to Secure Cyberspace, (Washington DC: The White House, February 2003)

[5] From introduction of history of Carl Philipp Gottfried (or Gottlieb) von Clausewitz, author unknown

[6] Danielle Reust, "Resource pool security procedures in a virtual infrastructure", November 2009, Resolution Enterprises Ltd.

[7] "The Machiavelli of Maryland", The Guardian online, Dec 9, 2015 (source: https://www.theguardian.com/world/2015/dec/09/edward-luttwak-machiavelli-of-maryland)

[8] Luttwak, Edward. Strategy: the logic of war and peace. Harvard University Press, 2001.

[9] Gartner; "Emerging Technology Analysis: Deception Techniques and Technologies Create Security Technology Business Opportunities" 16 July 2015 (updated 30 Sep 2016)

[10] Luttwak, Edward. Strategy: the logic of war and peace. Harvard University Press, 2001, p.6

[11] Ibid., p. 253

[12] From Introduction to history of Brigadier General Huba Wass de Czege, author unknown.

[13] Ibid.

[14] Image: DarkGovernment - 22 Jul 2011

[15] Joint Publication 3-13, Information Operations, (2012, November 27) with Change 1 (2014, November 20). Retrieved from http://www.dtic.mil/doctrine/new_pubs/jp3_13.pdf

[16] Ibid, Figure I-1, page I-2.

[17] Operations Security, US program since 1988, see
https://en.wikipedia.org/wiki/Operations_security

Towards the Design of an Interdisciplinary Bridge Curriculum in Health Information Systems: A Pilot Study

Niya Werts ★
nwerts@towson.edu

Subrata Acharya ★★
sacharya@towson.edu

Department of Health Science ★
Department of Computer and Information Sciences ★★
Towson University
8000 York Road, Towson, MD 21252

Abstract - This research responds to the critical need to develop educational opportunities to facilitate interdisciplinary communication and field literacy to better prepare students in the health sciences and technology fields for more effective inter-professional collaboration as well as next generation workforce development. The product of this research has been evaluated by an external focus group and can be used by educators in developing a framework for curriculum development, implementation, and evaluation of an interdisciplinary "bridge" course, and avoid some of the pitfalls of interdisciplinary course development.

Categories and Subject Descriptors

K.3.2 [Computers and Education]: *Governmental Issues – Regulation*

General Terms

Legal Aspect, Security, Privacy, Health Informatics

Keywords

Education, Health, Informatics, Security, University, Literacy

1   INTRODUCTION AND BACKGROUND

There are several documented barriers to successful adoption, implementation, and integration of value-adding information technology solutions in public health and health care settings [1][2]. The American Medical Informatics Association noted some of the primary barriers to successful implementation of health information systems were inter-professional communication and failure for stakeholders to understand the unique workflows of clinical environments [3]. Having translational knowledge across disciplines is an important part of professional success for health professionals working in technology intensive environments and/or informatics professionals specializing in health care systems. The literature supports the crucial role that "boundary spanning," [4] leaders and champions have in creating critical success factors for health information system integration [4][5]. Silos in curriculum development at the higher education level can reinforce the inability of future professionals to translate key concepts and knowledge to diverse stakeholders and hinder the ability to work effectively in interdisciplinary teams.

Interdisciplinary or Inter-professional education (IPE) education has been proposed as an important component in reducing medical errors in health care environments [6]. Likewise, inter-professional education, knowledge transfer and sharing in course curriculums could assist in meeting several key goals identified by the American Medical Informatics Association including building capacity in public health informatics, creating opportunities for informatics to develop broader perspectives on what public health is, and strengthening disease prevention efforts in the public health and clinical domains [7]. The goal of the pilot study course was to increase basic-intermediate level field content literacy across disciplines (health professions and technology) as a step towards better preparing budding health and informatics professionals for collaboration in health care and public health environments.

2   INTERDISCIPLINARY COUSE DESIGN FRAMEWORK

The course development and implementation process followed a logical progression based on the following steps: 1) Resource Allocation; 2) Identification of Core Curriculum Themes; 3) Course Implementation; 4) Course Evaluation.

2.1 Resource Allocation

This is a critical step in development of a new course, particularly one where faculty across different disciplines are required to collaborate. One must bear in mind that faculty members are resources to their respective departments, and each department and college within a university structure may differ in their priorities and procedures to utilize faculty resources.

There are several administrative issues to account for in the development and teaching of interdisciplinary courses, including departmental buy- in, determining faculty workloads, faculty salary, course titles, and course approvals. In order to come to an agreement on faculty workload, team teaching, and faculty salary to pilot the course, the authors met monthly for 3 months with relevant stakeholders in each Department to develop a formal proposal for the interdisciplinary course. The proposal included a literature based rationale for why exposing undergraduates to inter professional concepts in health and technology was a vital educational needs area, a regional market based overview of the employment prospects for those trained in health and informatics, and a sample syllabus. Both authors' departments were supportive of the course in theory, but could offer no additional financial support for faculty salaries to develop and teach the course. Authors were encouraged to apply for faculty funding from another school within the university that provides support for innovative course curricula and development. A proposal for the bridge course was finalized, submitted for review, and won a financial award for development and teaching. In total, the resource allocation for the bridge course took well over nine months.

2.1.1   Identification of Core Curricular Themes

Perhaps one of the biggest challenges in developing an interdisciplinary curriculum is determining what content best serves the needs of students with diverse academic, professional, and pre-professional backgrounds. After surveying the literature, the authors determined three core curricular thematic sequences: a) Human Factors in Health Care and Public Health Environments; b) Health Data Structures and Security; c) Health Care Technology Policies and Regulatory Issues.

a. Resistance to technology adoption in health environments is complex [2] and personal characteristics of the adopter and the adopter's environment are integral to understand if persons are to become effective champions for the role that technology can play in improving health outcomes at the clinical and public health levels. Knowledge of how health environments drive tasks, how people process and conduct those tasks, and how those tasks fit with technology is important for health it implementation [2].

b. Health data types, and security are foundation technology themes that create an accessible entry point into technology topics in the era of data driven and evidence based medicine and public health. Health data security was identified as an especially important topic that all students would need to be versed in. The goal of these lessons and lab assignments were to provide students the opportunity to analyze the present and emerging security technologies in health care and public environments. Students would be given demo sessions on the System Development Lifecycle and its relevance to the design of the domain systems. Some of the topics for the case assignments included, but were not limited to: Breach Analysis, Risk Assessment, Data De-Identification, Organizational Policy Analysis and Application and Operation Analysis.

c. Finally, tech policies and regulatory issues as it related to the Affordable Care Act's Meaningful use regulations, HITECH, HIPAA and the HITRUST and NIST framework and policies were the key content areas. The Affordable Care Act created industry wide incentives and a sense of urgency to implement health information technology across a variety of health settings. While public health data falls out of the specific purvey of the Affordable Care Act, public health is a rich source of data for medicine and public policy, thereby encouraging even integration of technology into public health databases even in the absence of current regulatory mandates.

After coming to agreement on the thematic sequences that needed to be explored in the content, the instructors created a final syllabus. Below is a sample of the weekly laboratory & course content including topics relevant to the interdisciplinary pilot course study:

- Public Health/Health Care Systems (Affordable Care, Meaningful Use, Regulations) Systems Development Lifecycle Overview and applications to public health and health care environments

- Data Driven Disease Tracking & Trends in Public Health Informatics

- Health Information Exchanges (Design and Implementation)

- Algorithms, Data Capture, Retrieval and Data Visualization

- Clinical Informatics (clinical decision support systems, nursing informatics)

- Basics Database Design (SQL and non-SQL database systems, queries)

- Medical Databases and Standards

- Personal Health Information Management (personal health apps)

- Tools and Technologies for Health Information Management

- Hybrid Medical Systems (Architectures and Frameworks)

- Quality, Usability and Standards

- International Healthcare Informatics

There is a gradual movement into the more complex data driven and data security topics with hands on labs to expose those students who have minimal exposure to these concepts and ensure students with technology backgrounds understood the specificity of health care hardware and software requirements.

2.1.2 Course Implementation

The course was piloted as a combined undergraduate and graduate course over a 10-week summer session. The maximum enrollment cap was set at 20 with 12 students enrolling. The course was team taught with two primary instructors from the respective departments (a health science department and a computer science department) with the instructors assigned to different weeks consistent with their field expertise. Additionally, guest speakers from the fields of epidemiology, nursing informatics, and personal health informatics presented during the course. A primary text authored by nurse informatics was identified and utilized. To assess student learning goal achievement, instructors implemented a variety of subjective and objective measures including objective exams, student presentations, and a group project designed to address a real-world IT in health care problem.

2.1.3 Course Evaluation

For the pilot, the standard university course evaluation was used to gather student quantitative and qualitative feedback. Additionally, instructors implemented a variety of subjective and objective measures including objective exams, student presentations, and a group project designed to assess student learning. To review process, the instructors met post course to review student evaluations, student feedback on the team teaching structure, and met with other instructors in both of their respective departments and stakeholders to discuss the outcomes of the pilot course and gather feedback for improvement. As part of the funding agreement, instructors also had to submit a comprehensive report to the internal funding school detailing the course implementation and student outcomes.

3   INTERDISCIPLINARY PILOT COURSE DEVELOPMENT: LESSONS LEARNED

3.1 Interdisciplinary courses require careful and target marketing

An interdisciplinary course will (in theory) work best when there is a diverse pool of students from different disciplines and backgrounds to both stimulate and simulate inter-professional dialogue and skill sharing. If a proposed course is not advertised well interdepartmentally, a skewness in student enrollment will alter the demographics of the class. In the pilot course, 10 of the 12 students were applied information technology students will little to no background in health concepts. Therefore, the ability to create balanced groups for in class discussion and the group project was not feasible. This skew in demographics also created challenges for the instructors who had to differentially scale the course content to support the lack of knowledge, and in some cases interest, in health concepts and the students' deficiencies in technology concepts relevant to health care, though they may have had strong academic knowledge in other aspects of technology. The lack of students from a health background was in part due to student fears that the technology topics would be beyond their scope of practice and abilities. The authors did not anticipate the importance of creating marketing materials that while conveying the clear intent of the class, were also crafted to allay technology fears for health professionals/ pre-professionals and emphasized the timely relevance of the health care topics to be discussed for technology professionals and pre-professionals. To address this issue, the authors strongly recommend that instructors prepare marketing materials specifically for their respective departments and disciplines rather than a one size fits all approach. Additionally, instructors will need to be very deliberate in the formation of in class student groups to avoid the "huddling effect" whereby students will naturally gravitate towards those in their respective disciplines.

3.1.1   Students career goals play a large role in student engagement

The pilot course revealed that undergraduate students with both low interest in healthcare as a career field and marginal technical skills performed below expectations on exam and project based assignments. However, at the graduate level students with either a previous health background and low technical skill, or an IT background with low previous healthcare knowledge performed above expectations in the course. These experiences emphasize the importance of student career goals (the healthcare field as primary or secondary career path) in course engagement and success. While the instructors decided to open the course for undergraduates and graduate to boost enrollment, it may have been more prudent to focus on early career graduate students rather than undergraduates. Persons pursuing post-baccalaureate, graduate, and professional education often have either a clear career advancement goal in mind and/or greater professional work experience that is advantageous in a course where communication across disciplines is a critical skill. Favorable qualitative feedback from graduate students (n=2) noted their levels of health, information technology, and the intersections therein expanded over the course of the semester.

3.1.2 Team Teaching and class structure should be modeled around inter-professional dialogue

Negative quantitative and qualitative feedback from some of the technology students that the course was too health-centric may reflect a missed opportunity and error on the part of the instructors. While the intent of the course was to mitigate silos, the course structure of alternating weeks to each instructor rather than collaborative teaching within the same session or week of the class seemed to both hurt student-teacher rapport, and the ability of the instructors to model the inter-professional dialogue so critical to the goals of the course. There are other alternative methods for co-teaching that could have effectively addressed student perception [8] including having both instructors present during some weeks to foster dialogue and highlight shared and divergent perspectives from both disciplines. Likewise, separating the academic topics rather than taking an integrated case- based approach to the course from the beginning, may not have served all students well. Students seemed to excel on innovative group project proposals including patient portals, proactive healthcare applications, emergency care service efficiency, and secure healthcare services. This implies that late in the course group collaboration was still successful despite the obstacles, and opens the door to consider alternative forms of case based learning, co-mentored by both faculty throughout course delivery. Team-based learning systems have already been well established in the health field, particularly nursing education [9], and may lend much needed structure to interdisciplinary education since the goals (heterogeneous team formation, student accountability, real world problem solving, and continuous feedback) [9] are the same.

3.1.3 Multiple types of student assessment should be conducted pre, midterm, and post

Interdisciplinary courses, like other courses, benefit from multiple levels of evaluation. Student evaluations provide some student feedback, but response rates for the pilot course were very low. Additionally, standard student evaluations only gave a dim snap shot of student course perceptions, and those perceptions ranged widely depending on student background. Beyond student perceptions, instructors need to further evaluate curriculum and process for interdisciplinary courses. Field literacy assessments, team teaching and group evaluation process assessments, and future and/or present employment job roles and responsibilities assessments be integrated into the evaluation milieu for interdisciplinary courses. Preliminary field literacy assessments are critical to better understand student knowledge levels in order for instructors to be able to scale the level of the subsequent course content weeks appropriately. Post-course field literacy assessments showing marked improvement across both disciplines help to support the contention that interdisciplinary courses can contribute to the creation of boundary spanning professionals. Team teaching and group evaluations should be administered mid-term and not only at the end. This will allow instructors to make any necessary course corrections early in the semester to better ensure the goals of the course are met. Assessing future and present desired employment job roles will allow instructors and relevant stakeholders to better match industry needs to the curriculum.

4   OUTCOMES OF THE PILOT STUDY

We conducted both formative and summative evaluation for the above pilot study. The students, faculty, curriculum design and external industry experts were active participants of the study. Because part of the impetus for the course was to be responsive to industry needs, three external industry experts from clinical fields (hospital and health care organizations) and one from the public health field (state government) participated in a focus group session to provide feedback on the bridge course syllabus, discuss the lessons learned from the pilot study, address industry relevance of several other interdisciplinary course initiatives, and determine next steps. Feedback from the industry evaluators was in general positive including indicating the employment categories most likely to benefit from these kind of courses (practicing health clinicians, data analysts, and federal employees). Industry evaluators also recommended strengthening the security and privacy curricular pieces within the bridge course and with other dedicated courses. Ultimately, industry evaluators and the internal funding school decided that a fully revised interdisciplinary course could serve as the first course within a 6-course sequence for a proposed post-baccalaureate certificate (PBC) program in Health Information Management. While the thematic sequences for the bridge course remain the same, revisions have been made in to address concerns about the target student market and curriculum alignment with regional health industry needs. Additionally, instructors will explore implementing an enhanced co-teaching structure and team based learning approaches. The revised course will also institute the formalized pre-and post-assessments identified to determine the efficacy of the course.

5   CONCLUSION

Interdisciplinary coursework in the field of health informatics presents challenges and opportunities to address the critical communication gaps that inhibit effective technology adoption in health care and public health settings. With the emerging need and intersection of technology in the improvement of cost and quality of healthcare systems, we believe the design and implementation of the proposed course will lead to the development of a well-prepared and able workforce to address the growing challenges for the 21st century. The PBC is planned to be disseminated at the graduate level through a cross-departmental program starting from Fall 2017. We plan to conduct rigorous periodic assessment of the progress of the program via employers' and external expert evaluator feedback, as well as student recruitment, retention and post study success to further enhance and expand the proposed program.

REFERENCES

[1] Leonard, K. J. Critical Success Factors Relating to Healthcare's Adoption of New Technology: A Guide to Increasing the Likelihood of Successful Implementation. Electronic Healthcare, 2(4) 72-81 (2004).

[2] Ammenwerth, E., Iller, C., & Mahler, C. IT-Adoption and the Interaction of Task, Technology and Individuals: A Fit Framework and a CaseSstudy. BMC Medical Informatics and Decision Making, 6(1) (2006).

[3] Kaplan, B., & Harris-Salamone, K. D. Health IT Success and Failure: Recommendations from Literature and an AMIA Workshop. Journal of the American Medical Informatics Association, 16(3) 291-299 (2009).

[4] Cresswell, K., & Sheikh, A. Organizational Issues in the Implementation and Adoption of Health Information Technology Innovations: An Interpretative Review. International Journal of Medical Informatics, 82(5) e73-e86 (2013).

[5] Bernstein, M. L., McCreless, T., & Cote, M. J. Five Constants of Information Technology Adoption in Healthcare. Hospital Topics, 85(1) 17-25 (2007).

[6] Blue, A. V., Mitcham, M., Smith, T., Raymond, J., & Greenberg, R. Changing the Future of Health Professions: Embedding Interprofessional Education within an Academic Health Center. Academic Medicine, 85(8) 1290-1295 (2010).

[7] Massoudi, B. L., Goodman, K. W., Gotham, I. J., Holmes, J. H., Lang, L., Miner, K., ... & Fu, P. C. An Informatics Agenda for Public Health: Summarized Recommendations from the 2011 AMIA PHI Conference. Journal of the American Medical Informatics Association, 19(5) 688-695 (2012).

[8] Perry, B., & Stewart, T. Insights into Effective Partnership in Interdisciplinary Team Teaching. System, 33(4) 563-573 (2005).

[9] Sisk, R. J. Team-based Learning: Systematic Research Review. Journal of Nursing Education, 50(12) 665-669 (2011).

Printed in Great Britain
by Amazon